THE NATURAL LAW
OF MONEY

WILLIAM BROUGH

COSIMO CLASSICS
NEW YORK

The Natural Law of Money

Cosimo
P.O. Box 416
Old Chelsea Station
New York, NY 10113-0416

or visit our website at:
www.cosimobooks.com

The Natural Law of Money originally published by Northeastern University Press in 1909.

Library of Congress Cataloging-in-Publication Data
A catalog record for this book is available from the Library of Congress

Cover design by www.wiselephant.com

ISBN: 1-59605-258-9

CONTENTS.

iii

CHAPTER III.

CHAPTER IV.

CHAPTER V.

Contents

THE NATURAL LAW OF MONEY

CHAPTER I.

THE BEGINNING OF MONEY.

IT may be well to explain at the outset what is meant to be conveyed by the phrase " the natural law of money." While it is true that money is a product of man's labor, and that it derives all its usefulness from the actions of men, it was not planned and brought into existence with an intelligent prevision of its nature and workings. It would be more correct to say that it came into use because it possessed inherent properties which fitted it for certain services, and that men appropriated it when they felt the need of the services. This they did individually, without any concert of action, for money was circulating everywhere in the world before men even thought of making laws for its regulation.

When an individual uses money, he is governed in what he does with it purely by his own interests, and he does not concern himself about what becomes of it after it passes out of his possession; thus it circulates indefinitely, impelled always by the motives and interests of individuals acting independently of each other; yet it is found to move and perform its functions with the regularity of a natural law.

The material of which money is composed may be almost any product of man's labor; it becomes money only when it is used as the common medium of exchange. Before the appearance of money in the world, exchanges of commodities were made in a very crude way. If a man had a dog that he wanted to exchange for a sheep, he could not make the exchange until he found some one who had a sheep and wanted a dog. But in the course of time man discovered that, among the commodities produced by him, there was always some one commodity in more general use and demand than others, and this he seized upon as his medium of exchange, —it became his money. Having done this, he was no longer obliged to wait until he found some one who had the particular commodity he wanted, and who also wanted his commodity; he stood ready to accept the commodity in general demand, because he could more readily exchange it for the commodity he wanted, and so, by a double turn, could save time and better accomplish his purpose.

This first way of making exchanges has been named barter, and the second, trade.

Here we see how money first came into use in the world. A great variety of articles has been appropriated for use as money at one time or another. We cannot mark the dates in history when these various commodities came to be used, as it was not the age, but the stage of development of the particular country, that created the need for them. We may find in the world to-day among primitive communities the crudest kinds of money that have ever been used. Step by step, and keeping even pace with increasing knowledge, have man's wants multiplied, and his implements for supplying those wants improved. He did not need money while he was hunting with his dog in the primeval forest, and living upon edibles already in existence; nor did he need it when he began to herd animals and to till the soil. Living in tribal isolation, and having no other bond of sympathy with his fellow-man than kinship, it was not until he was impelled by his necessities to exchange commodities with other tribes that he began to use money.

We can hardly overestimate the importance of money as a civilizing agent in the world; there can be no trade or commerce without it; man must have it, or go back to barbarism. By employing one of his commodities as a medium of exchange, he made a big stride forward; a new era was begun. His small beginnings were the seeds of the industrial progress we see around us. Impelled by want, producer meets producer, each having what the other needs for his own use or for the use of the tribal family; an exchange takes place, which is barter; and this form of traffic goes on increasingly until the need is felt for a medium of exchange; when that medium is found, man has become a trader. He has discovered that there is profit in these exchanges, and he no longer confines his trading to his immediate wants, but trades for profit as well. Every want that he satisfies stimulates into being other wants, and so his trading goes on increasing and extending. He has found in profit a new incentive to industry, a spur to continued exertion. But to succeed in his new occupation he must live in peace; his strength must not be wasted in the petty, but deadly, warfare he has hitherto carried on with neighboring tribes; he endeavors therefore to keep on good terms with them. He has already begun to add other ties to the bond of blood-relationship,—ties of self-interest, which grow gradually into friendship, into the merging of tribe with tribe, into a large political community, and finally into a nation.

We see from what has been said that man had no preconception of money: he felt the want of something, and the thing was ready to his hand,—a product of his own creating, but made for other uses. He appropriated it to supply the want, and so long as it was employed in that capacity, he called it " money."

In this brief outlining of the way in which money came into use, some things are to be especially noted and kept in mind. We have seen that money is a product of man's labor,—a commodity, and that it is not any one specific thing, but may be almost anything, and is money only by reason of its fitness at the time for the service to be performed. In any given community there is a limit to the number of articles produced, and in earlier times this limit was very much narrower than now; but however limited the number of commodities may be, there are always one or two that supply the money-want more efficiently than others. Now, as almost any commodity may be used as money, such a thing as a lack of it

is not possible so long as man continues to be a producer of commodities, although he may by false
legislation corrupt his money or throw restrictions
around it, and thus lessen its efficiency; all over the
world there have been examples of such false legislation whenever governments conceived it to be their
function to regulate the value of money.

Money fluctuates in value in sympathy with supply and demand, as all other commodities do. As
all values are relative, the only way to decide whether
money has risen or fallen is to compare it with other
commodities, and if the comparison covers several
years, the result will be all the more accurate. If it
is found that nearly all the staple commodities can be
bought with less money than formerly, we may be
sure that money has risen in value; if more is required, then it has fallen.

After adopting a commodity into use as money,
man begins to lose sight of its fluctuations in value;
these fluctuations appear to him to be altogether in
the commodities that he buys; he looks upon
money as stationary, and regards it as a fixed standard by which he can measure the value of other
commodities. Money is a definite measure, but not
a fixed measure, like a yard-stick. *There can be no
fixed measure for values.* As all values are relative,

it is only by comparing the price of one commodity with that of another that we get any idea of value; hence, to regard money as a fixed, and not as a fluctuating measure, produces the same kind of misconception that one would have of the solar system who regarded the earth as stationary. Until such delusions are dispelled, the one individual can no more understand the law of money than the other can realize the fact of the earth's orbit.

Since there can be no fixed measure for values, obviously it becomes of essential importance that the commodity selected for use as money should fluctuate as little as possible. The colonists of Virginia used tobacco as money until after the Revolution; there was always a ready sale for it, therefore people took it freely in exchange for other commodities; it was easily exchangeable for money or commodities in foreign as well as in the home markets. Wampum was used as money by the colonists of Massachusetts, not only in trading with the Indians, but for a short time among themselves, though only for limited amounts; it was the money of the Indians, and had no value to the colonist except as he might use it in trading with them, so it soon went out of use. As tobacco had intrinsic value and was readily exchangeable, it continued for a long time to be used as a medium of exchange; but as it was cumbersome and unsteady in price, it too went out of use. The commodity employed as money does not go out of use until it is superseded by one of superior qualifications for the service. This is the natural law that governs the change from one kind of money to another.

The fact that the Virginia colonist used tobacco as money was no indication of the stage of civilization he had reached; he merely used it to bridge over a period of scarcity of his own money,—which was silver, though gold was also in use in Virginia. His experience proves that if in our own case all our gold and silver were driven from the country, we should not be without money, though our new money would not have the efficiency of the old; we should have taken a step backward; while we would doubtless show great ingenuity in selecting new commodities for use as money, we should be in the position of a nation that had thrown away its improved tools and implements to take up those already cast aside. We might then accept the proposition of the Farmers' Alliance, and issue certificates against cattle, wheat, and corn, to be used as money. With the introduction of this money would come a new occupation, but an occupation without productiveness. Some of us would be detailed to go out and watch our new money, to see that the grain was not spoiling in the barns, and that pleuro-pneumonia had not got among the cattle. Our government might adopt excellent devices for the protection of this new money, but it could not prevent the sense of insecurity which pertains to a money of defective character. Should we adopt the Farmers' Alliance plan, it would not be the first time that cattle had done service as money. History records that this was the first form of money used in the world.

Wherever the metals came into use as money, they soon supplanted all perishable and clumsy commodities, being particularly adapted to such use, in which nearly all of them have done service at one time or another. They have great durability, being almost indestructible; they can be divided into convenient-sized pieces for handling and for the pocket, and can be run back into bars, if desired, without loss of value. The final test of coined money is that it shall be worth as much when run into bars as when it is in coin. If it will stand that test, it is world-money,—and all coined money should stand it. Coin in constant circulation loses value by abrasion, but this does not alter the rule; the loss from wear must be made good in return for the service rendered, or the coin will become discredited money. There is but one exception to the otherwise inflexible rule that coin shall possess full intrinsic value, and that is as to the small coin used for change ; this is purposely made light in order to keep it at home. In speaking of coin, or money, this *change-money* or *token-money*, will not be again referred to, unless specifically mentioned.

We have seen that wherever metallic money came into use, it displaced all the cruder forms of money. But the line of advance did not end there. One metal displaced another, the incoming one always having greater efficiency than the outgoing one. Copper was the money of Rome in her earlier days, and is the legal money of China to-day. If we could know all the forms of money in the world, we should doubtless find that the baser metals are still in use in some places. The order of progress is that each in turn shall drop out of use as money, and be put to other uses for which it is better fitted. The ever-increasing demand for more things and better things, calls for better implements and more and more intelligent methods of workmanship. The forces that control this movement are beyond our reach, as we shall do well to recognize, and so bring our feeble attempts at monetary legislation into harmony with them, instead of struggling to overcome them. If silver is now going out of use as money, in the natural way, we must let it go; we cannot stay it, and the attempt to do so can only involve us in trouble. If, when iron was in use as money, man had piled it away in vaults—as we have done with silver—and had kept it out of other uses, is it not plain that his action would have retarded the progress of civilization?

In the development of a money adapted to the wants of man, silver and gold have come to be the money metals of the most advanced nations. The superior efficiency of these metals has been established by ages of use, but their qualifications are different. In the earlier stages of mercantile enterprise, silver sufficed for all the requirements of trade, but it proved inadequate to the demands and exigencies of that larger and more complex trade which we call *commerce*. Gold met these requirements more effectively, and it has become the money of commerce. The monetary similarity of silver and gold prevents the rapid displacement of the one metal by the other, while their monetary differences make both the metals useful at the same time in one country; so that we find silver retained in use by nations like England and

Germany, though gold is the monetary standard. Indeed, it is hard to see how any nation could altogether discontinue the use of silver as money.

Gold has always been more valuable than silver, hence less time is required to weigh or to count a given amount in gold, and when money has to be transported from one place to another, the carriage of gold costs less. It is because of such nice differences as these that the changes from one money to another have taken place, man always seizing upon the agency that will most effectually serve his purpose and supply his need. Without gold, it would now be hardly possible to transact the volume of business that is done in the world. To be compelled to use only silver money would be a check upon enterprise and a burden to commerce.

If a nation that had reached the gold stage of industrial development should adopt the single silver standard, it would surely be at a disadvantage in its commercial transactions with gold-standard nations. Silver is not only more cumbersome than gold, but has always been more fluctuating—of late years much more so than formerly. If we should adopt the single silver standard, it would put us on the monetary basis of Mexico and Russia ; with these nations we should be at no disadvantage in our commercial intercourse, but with such nations as England, France and Germany we should be at great disadvantage. In their dealings with us, they would charge us for the risk they incurred in accepting a less stable money than their own; this charge would be added to the cost of goods imported, and deducted from the price of goods exported by us. It would not only increase the cost of our imports and reduce the price of our exports, but it would also reduce the price at home of all those commodities of which we produce a surplus; our entire products of cotton and of wheat, for example, would be measurably lowered in price. Everybody knows that when the price of wheat goes up or down abroad, it correspondingly rises or falls at home, for the price at home is governed by the price that we can get for the surplus that goes abroad. The risk from fluctuations of our silver money would be as constantly present in all commercial transactions with gold-money countries as is the risk of the sea-carriage, and would have to be insured against in the same manner, with the difference only that in the case of the sea-risk the cost is borne equally by the buyer and the seller, whereas in the case of our fluctuating money the cost would fall entirely upon us.

In order to render to man the highest service of

which it is capable, metallic money must have *intrinsic value*, *stability*, and *elasticity*.

The fundamental requisite of metallic money is that it shall have full intrinsic value. From the beginning of money, through all its forms down to the introduction of paper-money, this rule has governed inflexibly at all times, except when abrogated or interfered with by rulers and law-makers. The term "intrinsic value," as here used, means that a coin contains its full denominational worth of precious metal; in other words, that its nominal and its actual exchangeable values are the same. If coin contains its full complement of precious metal when issued from the mint, and if its free circulation be not thereafter interfered with, it will have intrinsic value, which, combined with freedom of circulation, will give it stability and elasticity.

The *stability* of coin must rest upon the value of the bullion it contains, as then it will fluctuate only with the fluctuations of the bullion market, which is the highest degree of steadiness it can possibly acquire. It will then gain access to the marts of the world, and this wide range of circuit will enhance its "elasticity," which term is used to express the readiness with which money responds to the demands upon it. The importance of this quality in money will be treated in more detail when we come to speak of paper-money.

It is obvious that the larger, broader, and more open the market for any commodity, the more steady will be the price of that commodity. These are marked characteristics of the bullion market; consequently, to give to coin all the elements of efficiency it can possess, it is only necessary to start it into circulation with its full weight and fineness of precious metal, and let it go where it will. Here we have the natural law of *metallic money* in all its simplicity; the complexities are of our own making.

The miner of California in 1849 made his purchases with gold dust, weighing it in scales. It was thus, doubtless, that the metals were measured when they first came into use as money. In coining money for the people, our government performs a very important service; the bullion is minted in convenient forms for handling and for expressing value, thus dispensing with scales and saving time; but the service rendered has a still higher significance. The stamp of the government is a sufficient assurance that the coin contains the required amount of the precious metal: if coining were left to individuals, there would arise doubt on that score that would greatly lessen the efficiency of the money.

If money is to be efficient, there must be no uncertainty as to its quality, for the questioning doubt will limit its usefulness. A sense of security gives mobility to money, and the lack of that sense cripples it. No intelligent community was ever deceived by debased money; nor has there ever been a community so ignorant that it would not in course of time discover the deception. Emerson has said that not even a tree is so stupid but that if the earth is taken from its roots, it will find it out.

Following this line of thought, we perceive that it was the questioning doubt that led to the coinage of metals; for, as the operation of assaying is both difficult and tedious, it would become necessary, in order to facilitate exchanges, that the operation should be performed and verified by an unquestioned authority; and this work the people would naturally require their government to do for them. We know that it was the fineness, not the weight, of the metal that was stamped on the first rude coins, the people weighing them for themselves in making their exchanges. The next improvement in coinage was to stamp the weight on the coins, and these pieces were designated by their weight. The Roman "pondo" was a pound of copper, the English "pound" a pound of silver, and the English "penny" a pennyweight of silver. Money passed from hand to hand by tale; but when a large sum was to be transferred, it was weighed, because that could be done more easily and accurately. The practice of weighing large amounts of coin still prevails.

The next step in coinage was a step backward. The coinage came to be known as "king's money"; it bore the effigy of the sovereign, and the pieces were more artistically minted; but they were given names that had no reference to their weight or fineness. This irrelevant naming was misleading, and people soon lost sight of money as a commodity, and came to regard the stamp and denomination as its valuable part. The superstitious awe in which kings were then held made it but a short step from the belief that a king's touch would cure disease, to the belief that his effigy and superscription gave value to the coin. By this last change in coin, which obliterated the meaning of money, the people lost control of their coinage,—that control had passed into the hands of the kings. Let us see what they did with it.

It may be stated as an axiom that, down to modern times, kings have been lavish and wasteful in their expenditures, and that, with few exceptions, they have been governed altogether by cupidity in

2

their dealings with their subjects; these were kept in a constant conflict with their rulers to retain in rightful possession the product of their toil and labor; the one power that should have protected them in that right, was the power they dreaded most. The long conflict developed into a struggle for political supremacy, and while it went on, the wealth-producing capacity of the people was maintained or diminished in proportion as the contest went in their favor or against them.   When resistance to the demand of the ruler ceased altogether, the people sank into poverty and serfdom; when this resistance was successful, the people rose to affluence and political independence.   The people of England, after a long monetary struggle with their kings, succeeded in appropriating to themselves exclusive control of the revenues and expenditures of the kingdom; the coining of money continued to be a prerogative of the king, but gradually it came under the direction, and finally under the absolute control, of Parliament.

A common and favorite method adopted by rulers to raise money was to abstract from the coinage a portion of its precious metal, and to substitute therefor a cheaper metal; when resistance was made to receiving such money, its circulation was enforced by mandate.   This doubtless seemed to the rulers a ready road to wealth, but nothing could have been

more destructive of the prosperity of their people,
or of their own prosperity. A debased coinage
seems to have entered into the experience of every
civilized nation at some period of its history. Among
the Romans, the pondo decreased to a half ounce of
copper, in England the pound sterling to less than
one-third of a pound of silver, and some coins in
Scotland were reduced to less than one-sixtieth of
their normal value. That the rulers have been
chiefly responsible for this debasement will be seen
when we come to consider the Gresham law.

There is an interesting chapter in Macaulay's *History of England* which describes how the clipping and
sweating of coin gradually so lowered the standard
of money as to bring great distress upon the nation.
This was in the time of William III.; the vigorous
and intelligent action of Parliament corrected the
evil; no less a personage than Sir Isaac Newton was
appointed Warden of the Mint, while the famous
philosopher John Locke expounded his theory of
money.

We have long ceased to regard the king's person
as more sacred than that of a subject; nevertheless,
a remnant of that old superstitious belief in the
potency of sovereignty found its way to the New
World, and is here with us still, to tangle our thoughts
and blur our perceptions.

CHAPTER II.

BI-METALLISM AND MONO-METALLISM.

IN calling our silver and gold coins by the same
name, " dollar," and in trying to hold them at
an equal value under a fixed ratio, is there not evidence of a lingering belief that the power of sovereignty can regulate the value of coin? And is not
the effort to enforce the circulation of the two coins
at equivalent value a survival of the king's mandate
in modified form? Have we not overlooked the fact
that silver and gold are commodities, the values of
which are regulated only in one way, and by the
same rule that regulates the value of other commodities—by letting them find in open market what
that value is? They are not alike, not even in their
money functions. They are both metals, to be sure,
as wheat and barley are both cereals: what more
cogent reason is there for making silver and gold an
equivalent tender than for making wheat and barley

an equivalent tender? Is it not evident that we have inherited from the past a vague notion that we can, in some mystic manner, regulate the value of our metallic money? If a legislative enactment could confer that power, similar legislation would enable us to regulate the value of all our commodities.

The well-meant efforts to hold silver and gold coin at a parity in value have had no other effect than to drive one of these metals out of active current service. This has been our experience from the beginning of our government down to this day. We have not had both coins in circulation simultaneously, except during the short intervals when one was going out and the other coming in, and all other nations have shared this experience. Whenever the metals composing the two coins are put up for sale in open market, the price of each is governed by the supply of and demand for each; in no other way can their true value be ascertained; each must stand on its own merits. The efforts of governments to give them equality in value seem to have had the opposite effect.

It is estimated that three-fifths of the volume of silver and gold in the world are used in the arts, and two-fifths in money; but this is only an estimate— accurate figures cannot be had. That the amount of these metals used as money is sufficiently large to considerably affect their market value is, however, a matter of course ; but that the efforts to hold them at a relatively fixed value have utterly failed, is proved by the whole history of bi-metallism.

All the leading commercial nations at one time or another have tried to harness these two money-metals together, and make of them one monetary standard. We may suppose the first step towards this end to be the determining of the amount of silver and of gold respectively that shall constitute coins of equal value, the ratio being adjusted to the relative market value of these metals at the time. The act authorizing this coinage would also make the silver and gold coin an equivalent tender at the ratio fixed. This is what is termed *bi-metallism.* In course of time, the market values of the two metals part company ; one may go up or the other down, or they may move simultaneously in opposite directions. As soon as this separation takes place, the coin of the metal which has risen in value begins to disappear from the circulation. This movement, unlike the intelligent order of free selection (in which the superior money supersedes the inferior), has nothing to do with the inherent fitness of the metals for ser-vice as money ; indeed, the coin going out of circulation may be the more serviceable money for the time and place; it disappears only because it is worth more as bullion than the coin remaining in circulation.

The mode of operation whereby, contrary to the law of natural displacement, an inferior money may expel a superior money from the circulation, is known as the Gresham law, and is so called because first expounded by Sir Thomas Gresham, who lived in the sixteenth century, and who was the founder of the Royal Exchange of London. The Gresham law would never have been heard of had coin passed by weight only, because in that case the recipient would have taken the coin only at the market value of the precious metal it contained; but when coin became king's money and people were required to accept it by tale at its face value, objection was made to pieces that did not contain the full complement of precious metal; as, however, the king's money was mandatory, it could not be refused so long as his imprint remained upon the coin. The fact that coin could not be refused—whether it contained the full complement of precious metal or not—was practically an invitation to every holder of a coin to abstract some metal from it before passing it, and this was practised to such an extent in England that in course of time, and by slow degrees, the whole coinage of the realm was reduced to about two-thirds of its standard weight and value.

As nothing is more destructive of industrial prosperity than a money of indefinite value, this continuous mutilation of the coinage finally involved the nation in intolerable distress, and how to restore the coinage to its normal standard was a problem the solution of which long puzzled the people of England. The belief was general that if the full-weight coin were put into circulation, it would of itself, as being a more desirable money, drive the light-weight coin out of use; and this view seemed all the more reasonable in that the people were unanimous in demanding of their government a reformation of the coinage.

But this view did not take into account the natural forces that control the circulation of money, nor did it recognize the personal character of money, and its relationship to the individual; it regarded money only from the public stand-point—as an impersonal agency. As all the transformations and movements of money take place naturally, through individuals acting separately and independently, each one in his own interest, and without any purpose to further a general law, we must recognize this personal and private interest as the real and only means whereby the coinage could be restored to, and preserved in, its normal integrity. So long as the king's effigy was the important factor, individuals continued to abstract from the coin any metal that could be taken without impairment of the effigy; but if the law were repealed which gave the king's effigy the quality of money, the coin would be taken only at its bullion market value. Each individual, acting for himself, without the least reference to the public interest, would refuse to receive the coin on any other terms, which would at once put a stop to any further debasement of the coinage.

As then there could be no further profit in the clipping and sweating of coin, clipping and sweating would cease; the debased coin at its bullion market value would be as good money intrinsically as that which came fresh from the mint, but as the clipped pieces would be of different values and intrinsically below their nominal value, they could be used in trade only by weighing them. Hence the same individual interest that had formerly led to the debasement of the coinage would now require that the pieces be made of uniform weight and fineness for the greater convenience of counting them and of expressing value.

In thus minutely defining the means by which a debased coinage could be restored, our object is to call especial attention to the fact that the debasement of the money was caused solely by its legal-tender quality, and that its restoration and preservation could only be effected by the removal of that cause. Nothing more was needed, because, as soon as the money was deprived of its legal-tender feature, it came under the law of natural displacement, and under this law, it is only the money of *superior efficiency* that can maintain supremacy in the circulation; whereas, when the artificial quality of legal-tender is given to money, it is always the *cheaper* money that expels the money of *higher value*, without the least reference to the efficiency of either.

The English government was finally enabled to restore the coinage by decreeing that clipped coin should pass by weight only, thus virtually repealing its legal-tender quality; but before taking this step the government had confidently expected to accomplish its purpose simply by recoining the mutilated pieces. As the government received the clipped coin at its full nominal value, and as the people were consequently eager to obtain the new money in exchange for their clipped money, it was taken for granted that the coinage could be re-established within a short time by increasing the output of the mints; and this was accordingly done. Much of the coin in circulation had been minted by hand, with shears and hammer, at earlier dates than the time now referred to, which is 1695–6; these pieces were so rudely formed that the edges could be clipped without detection; but as the new coin was minted with milled edges, to clip it was a more hazardous undertaking, and this strengthened the public confidence that a sound currency would soon be established.

Meantime, the law against clipping was vigorously enforced; counterfeiting had long been punished with the same extreme penalties as treason, and in the reign of Elizabeth the clipping of coin was also made a capital offence. Besides the clipped silver money, there were also in circulation at that time gold pieces issued in the reign of Henry VIII., which had been debased by that monarch to half their nominal value, and it is to this gold coin that Sir Thomas Gresham especially referred in expounding his law, which he did in a letter to Queen Elizabeth, written in the year 1558. Though he explained the practical working of the debased money, showing clearly how it drove the full-weight coin of Elizabeth from the circulation and from the country, he did not suspect the real cause of the evil, which was the mandatory character of the debased coin. He noted in this letter the disadvantage which the English merchants labored under in their exchanges with the continent—for it is in a foreign country that the coin of a nation must surely answer the test of bullion value. The superstitious awe that hedged a king in his own country had no influence upon the value of his coin when that coin went abroad ; nor were the Jews, who were the principal dealers in money and bills of exchange, in the least misled by the king's image on the coin.

A persecuted and plundered race, everywhere in Europe denied the right of ownership in real estate, the Jews had no avenue of commercial activity save the dealing in such personal property as could easily be secreted ; thus they found their recompense in the establishment of a monopoly of the most lucrative of trades. Themselves freed from monetary delusions, their course as money-changers operated as a constant protest against the debasement of the coinage, and so contributed to raise the standard of monetary integrity.

The English government having in 1695 entered seriously upon a reform of the coinage by practically giving full weight for light-weight pieces, while at the same time requiring that both full- and light-weight pieces should circulate at their nominal value, and there being no doubt in the public mind as to the ultimate success of this measure, attention was naturally fixed upon the circulation to note the process of change from the old money to the new. Great was the disappointment when, after large sums of the new money had been coined and paid out, there was no perceptible increase of new pieces in the circulation ; they vanished almost as fast as they came from the mint.   The financiers and the politicians of that age seem alike to have expected that the new money would soon displace the old, and, as Macaulay has said, they " marvelled exceedingly that everybody should be so perverse as to use light money in preference to good money."

But it was really everybody's preference for the full-weight pieces that kept these pieces out of the circulation, for, as their bullion value was half as much more than the bullion value of the clipped pieces, each person who received a good piece naturally held it and paid out his clipped money.   Each naturally sought to appropriate the extra value that the new coin possessed, and this he could do in several ways : he could melt it and sell it as bullion ; he could abstract the extra value from it by paring it down before passing it ; or he could hoard it until he found opportunity to pass it at its actual bullion value. All these things were done ; but that the rapid disappearance of the new coin from the circulation arose mainly from hoarding by the people who could afford to hoard, was afterwards shown by its reappearance when the government decreed that the clipped coin should no longer pass as money.

For at least a hundred years clipping had been a capital offence ; a law was now enacted against melting or exporting coin, but it could not be enforced ; nor could hoarding be prevented ; even the laws against clipping were ineffective, notwithstanding the terrible punishments inflicted upon offenders. Macaulay narrates that in one day seven men were hanged and one woman burned for clipping, yet the number of clippers multiplied in proportion as the volume of new coin thrown into the currency increased ; which demonstrates not only the futility of governmental regulation of a people's money, but its utterly demoralizing effect upon money and people alike. Harsh as was the law against the crime of clipping, it was even more unjust than harsh, for, in compelling the acceptance of debased coin at its nominal rather than at its actual value, the government was in fact an abettor of the crime it was seeking to suppress.

Although the English government, by demonetizing the clipped coin, was enabled to restore the
coinage, this action was not prompted by any intelligent perception of the real cause of the debasement,
but came upon government and people alike as a
dynamic necessity. We have seen that it was the
legal-tender quality of the coin that caused its debasement, and that if it had been deprived of this
quality, individual interest and action would have
restored and preserved the coinage in its integrity ;
but as it was the general belief that money circulated
only through the mandatory authority of the Crown,
this simple, natural law of money was not perceived.
In other words, the trying experience of the English
people with their clipped coin did not dispel the delusive idea that the Crown could regulate the value
of money ; in the belief of the people, the clipped
coin ceased to pass because the decree had gone out
that it should not pass, and the sound coin passed
because the decree had gone out that it should pass.

The same Parliament which decreed that the
clipped coin should not pass, also made it a penal
offence to give or take more than twenty-two shillings for a guinea, which is conclusive evidence that
this Parliament believed in the power of sovereignty
to regulate the value of the coin.   Silver was then

the predominant money ; it was this metal that was the common medium of exchange and measure of values, gold occupying a secondary place. The name " guinea " is still used in England to express twenty-one shillings, though the coin is no longer minted or in circulation ; the actual value of these gold pieces then, as measured by the new silver pieces, was twenty-one shillings and sixpence, but before the coinage was restored, their exchangeable value, as measured by the clipped money, was about thirty shillings. Though the clipped money could not be made to pass current at its nominal value, it did pass for more than its actual bullion value, for the reason that the government accepted it at its nominal value for the payment of taxes. The decree of Parliament in reference to the guinea was supererogatory legislation, as, after the restoration of the coinage, this piece passed at its normal value of twenty-one shillings and sixpence.

In the act of Parliament which undertook to hold the gold guinea in circulation at a fixed silver valuation, is plainly indicated the mandatory theory of money which, twenty-one years later (1717), led England to adopt bi-metallism, and which has more or less influenced her monetary legislation down to the present time. After nearly a century's practical experience with bi-metallism, England abandoned it for mono-metallism ; gold meantime having become the dominant metal, was made her monetary standard.

The course taken by England with her metallic money, and which has been followed by some of the chief commercial nations of Europe, may be briefly stated thus : bi-metallism has first been adopted ; then, after experience has shown that the silver and the gold coin cannot be held at a parity, the law which was designed to make one monetary standard out of two independent money metals, has been repealed ; the metal found to be the less serviceable has been discarded, and the other by enactment made the only legal tender, thus creating what is called *mono-metallism*. Whilst mono-metallism is undoubtedly an advance upon bi-metallism, inasmuch as it furnishes a more definite monetary standard, both systems embody the mandatory theory, and interfere with the natural flow of money.

Although the mandatory theory of money is still acted upon, even by the most advanced governments, it is gradually yielding to the pressure of natural forces. This is shown especially in their coinage legislation.   Except in bi-metallic countries, no attempt is now made to enforce the circulation of coin on any other basis than its intrinsic value ;

3

the pieces are by most nations made a legal tender at a full and a short weight, the difference between these weights being very slight, and designed only to provide a margin for the ordinary abrasion from a reasonable length of service. When a piece falls below its short weight it ceases to be a legal tender.

There is really no more occasion for a legal tender short weight in coin than there is for a legal tender short weight in the pound-weight. A moment's reflection will show that the tendency of such legislation by inciting fraudulent abrasion, is to degrade coin to the lowest level at which it may be tendered. It is estimated that of the gold in the currency of England, one-half the pieces, amounting to fifty million pounds, are barely above their short weight. Higgling over short-weight pieces is not uncommon there, although this is precisely what the long and short weight is intended to obviate.

In our own country, coin enters so sparingly into the general circulation that the deterioration from natural wear is very much slower than in England, and the short weight is so nicely adjusted to the natural wear by our Coinage Act of 1873, that there is practically no temptation to fraudulent abrasion.

Clearly there is no need of making coin a legal

tender at any specified weight. If governments would confine their legislation to fixing by enactment the fineness of the precious metal and the number of grains that shall constitute each piece of a given name, they may safely leave the maintenance of the coinage in its integrity, and the value of the pieces, to be regulated by individual interest and action. In practice this point of monetary advancement has been reached by most of the civilized nations; but in the useless, although comparatively harmless act of decreeing coin a tender at the authorized legal weight only, is manifested the extreme conservatism which still clings to the old delusion that legislation may in some vague sense regulate the value of coin.

Although this delusion is harmless as embodied in many coinage acts, it becomes extremely mischievous when the attempt is made to regulate the value of the silver and gold coin at a fixed ratio of weights under the ruling of bi-metallism; and it is only in a less degree mischievous when one of the money metals is ejected from the circulation under the ruling of mono-metallism. As the efficiency of coin as a medium of exchange depends on its circulating only at its bullion market value, and on the freedom with which it may circulate, any attempt to interfere with these natural conditions operates as a restriction of individual rights.

A government can render most important service by assaying the precious metals and minting the coin, by verifying the fineness and weight of the pieces, by guarding the coin against criminal deterioration, and by shaping the pieces in accordance with the actual needs of the time. More than this no government can do without trenching upon the freedom of the money, and, as a consequence, upon the rights of the individual, for his rights are bound up with his money, and his money, be it ever so sound, must have freedom to render him its most efficient service.

Money is identified with man as an individual, and not with man in mass; it is through the individual acting independently that it acquires all its potency. Moved by the incentive of gain, and for the gratification of his desires, the individual works only for himself and for those who come within the compass of his affections. It is by such delicate, complex, and hidden relationships to the individual that money becomes the circulating medium of a nation; and as the free circulation of the blood vivifies the body, so the unrestricted circulation of money vivifies the nation. If governments had limited their legislation to the simple requirements mentioned above, Sir Thomas Gresham would have had no occasion to expound the law that inverts the order of natural selection and drives money from circulation regardless of its efficiency ; nor would we have any silver question to discuss ; the two metals might then circulate as efficient money in one country at the same time ; if one went out of use, it would be because it was no longer needed and could do better service in other occupations ; the transition would be quiet and without disturbance to industry.

Let us now make an application of the principles of money to the actual workings of bi-metallism, as exemplified by the experience of our own and other nations. It has been shown that money may be any commodity that is used as the common medium of exchange, which is money only when so used. From the beginning of trade down to the introduction of paper-money, commodities employed as money necessarily possessed for that use full intrinsic value, except when kings, clippers, or sweaters abstracted a part of that value, or when law-makers undertook to create a factitious value. Although the money of the Massachusetts Indians had no value to the colonists, we need not doubt that it had real value to the Indians ; that is, it had cost them as much to produce as they could get for it. The colonists counterfeited this money, which they would hardly have done if they could have produced the genuine more cheaply than they could obtain it through trade. It has also been shown that silver and gold, through a series of displacements, proved themselves better qualified for monetary service than all other commodities, and so came into use wherever a people had risen high enough in industrial civilization to appreciate this superiority. It has also been shown that silver and gold differ in their monetary functions, the first being adapted to trade, while the second performs the larger and more complex duties of commerce; and when we extend our inquiries to paper-money, we shall see that its functions differ from those of silver and gold; that it is an implement of higher refinement than either, performing more complex duties; that it is, in short, the money of a still higher civilization, requiring for its most effective working a higher intelligence and a higher degree of integrity. It has also been shown that metallic money acquires its highest efficiency when left perfectly free to find its actual value in open market.

The open market here referred to really represents the whole world, for the precious metals are everywhere in use and everywhere bought and sold; it not only embraces the accumulations of all former ages, but receives the entire current product of these metals, which is continuously pouring into it. While we cannot compute either the amount of the precious metals in the world, or the amount required for the many different uses to which they are applied, we can easily see that fortunately this market is too large, and broad, and free, to be brought under governmental control; if it were not so, the useful-ness of the metals for money service would surely be paralyzed or destroyed. In the magnitude and freedom of this market, in the constantly changing form of the metals as they pass from one use to another, a continuous movement is kept up, and an even poise is preserved by innumerable buyings and sellings. Every change that peoples may make in their money, every transaction in trade and com-merce, wherever made, touches and influences to some extent this wonderful market.

A little thoughtful study of this market should suffice to show that the bi-metallic theory of money is a mistake. A slight change in the market value of silver and gold from the ratio fixed by law will drive one of these metals out of monetary service; and the only effect of an effort to retain both by making the coins interchangeable will be to impose upon one the burden of carrying the other.

England adopted bi-metallism in 1717, and changed to mono-metallism in 1816, selecting gold as her standard. Germany made a similar change in 1871, and her example was followed by Norway, Sweden, Denmark, and our own country, all within three years. But there is no evidence that these nations were prompted in their action by the fear of an approaching decline in silver, or by any other desire than to secure a more stable standard of money. The price of silver had not materially fallen at the time these changes were made, nor had the output of the silver mines increased to any marked degree, as they did later; so that no one could have had any reason to suppose that silver would fall in price, as it subsequently did.

By demonetizing silver in 1873, we doubtless helped to strengthen the general movement towards mono-metallism, but in no other way could our action have had any effect on the price of silver, as for about thirty years there had been practically no silver dollars in our circulation, and in 1873 we were on a paper-money basis. That our subsequent action, in passing the Silver Bill of 1878 had a depressing effect on the silver market, is more than probable; it was regarded by the world at large as an effort to give to the metal an artificial value, and this impression created a distrust that greatly restricted the freedom of the market. An attempt made a few years ago to control the copper market of the world created a similar distrust, which had the effect of putting the price of copper below its normal level, as was plainly seen when the syndicate, which had attempted to advance the price, broke down in bankruptcy, thus putting a stop to its interference.

France has done more than any other nation to maintain the double standard; her bankers and economists have been strong supporters of this monetary theory; five other nations co-operate with her, composing what is termed the Latin Union; yet in all these countries, if there is not a premium on, there will be a preference for, one of the metals; and even a preference is sufficient to lessen the usefulness of both. France closed her mints against free coinage of silver in 1876, and it is quite evident from the way in which she is accumulating gold and discarding silver, that she is moving toward a monometallic standard.

There is a limit to the amount of money that any community can employ productively, and what that limit is can never be measured mechanically.   If the money metals are left free to flow in and out of a country, their supply will be self-regulating, and every legitimate demand for metallic money will be met.   If the supply of these metals in the world at large is at any given time insufficient to meet the demand, there will necessarily be an appreciation in the value of money; if, on the other hand, the supply is in excess of the demand, money will depreciate.   These fluctuations are constantly occurring, but they are so slight as to be hardly noticeable.   In reviewing a long period of time, however, we find that the general tendency is towards lower values, and this applies not only to the precious metals, but to all products of man's labor.   Since the introduction of steam power, machinery, and subdivision of labor, the tendency towards lower prices has been more decided than before.   To obtain a more abundant supply of the necessaries, comforts, and luxuries of life, is the object of all industry, and with the increase of supply comes the reduction in price. This is the natural order of progress, of civilization.

As nearly as we can now judge, the decline in value of the precious metals has kept comparatively even pace with the decline in prices of commodities. There have been but two marked exceptions to this rule, arising from natural causes; one when Europeans got possession of Mexico and Peru, and the other when the gold fields of California and Australia were opened. In the latter case there was a depreciation in the price of gold; this was made evident by a general advance in the price of commodities, including silver, all over the civilized world. It was not until 1879 that gold recovered the value that it had had, as compared with other commodities, before 1850.

If England, instead of demonetizing silver in 1816, had permitted her silver and gold coin to circulate independently, and if the other European nations had followed this example, both metals would have circulated freely in all these countries, and with much slighter fluctuations, and the people would have been perfectly competent, in making their exchanges, to adjust them to the two monetary standards.

There has been too much legislative interference with money, and the best we can do now is to recognize this and act accordingly. In a country like ours, there can never be a lack of efficient money, if we observe the natural law of money; our immense natural resources and the industry of our people are a guaranty against it. We have now a superabundance of money that does not properly perform its functions.   Gold is practically our standard, but it is burdened with carrying silver, whereby the efficiency of both metals is reduced; nor does it alter these conditions to issue silver in the form of paper-money.   The silver in the Treasury vaults is of no more use to us now than when it was in its native hills.   Nobody questions the capability of the United States to redeem any obligation it may assume; the only question that has been raised in reference to our silver money is, what is its value? And this is a point upon which there should never be any room for doubt.

Two examples have been given showing how one money may replace another in the circulation; the first was the natural order of displacement, whereby the more serviceable money displaces a less serviceable money; the second was the artificial displacement that occurs under bi-metallism, when the cheaper money drives the more valuable money from the circulation.   It remained for the United States to give a third example of displacement, which, like the second, was artificial.   It was furnished by the silver legislation of 1878 and 1890, by which there was injected monthly into the currency a specified amount of silver.   This feature of the legislation was a monetary anomaly; nothing of the kind had ever been attempted before. It worked upon what is called the "per capita" plan—so many heads, and so many dollars per head. Machinery was set in motion to grind out a given number of dollars per month, and the country was forced to take them and pay for them, whether it needed them or not. There is a limit to the amount of money that any community can employ productively; therefore, to force money into the circulation after that limit is reached, is to force other money out. It will be seen that in this third example the displacement is purely mechanical, and without reference either to serviceableness, as in the first example, or to value, as in the second; the money goes simply because it is not needed.

Having thus stated the three forms of monetary displacement, we will now consider them somewhat more specifically, as exemplified by the operation of the acts referred to, especially that of 1890, commonly called the Sherman Act. We have seen that while money may be mechanically forced into the circulation, it cannot be retained there unless there is employment for it. The country has had a practical illustration of this in the necessary retirement of a large volume of national-bank notes, though these notes were practically the same in efficiency and value as the silver notes supplied by the government.   Many of the banks found a little more profit in redeeming their own notes and using the government notes instead, but this profit was not in itself sufficient to induce them to retire their notes if there had not already been an excess in the volume of the currency.   That this was so is shown by the fact that much of this retired money reappeared when the volume of the circulation was reduced by the paper-money hoarding which began in the summer of 1893.

Though the national-bank notes were displaced by this mechanical enlargement of the volume of currency, the gold money which retired was not similarly displaced ; nor would it have retired from the circulation had it not been for the Act of 1890, by which Congress sought to give it a silver valuation below its bullion market value.   But for this mandatory decree, gold money would, by reason of its superior efficiency, have remained in circulation to the exclusion of silver money when the volume of currency was in excess of the needs.   The silver dollar has continued to pass at a parity with the gold dollar, but this has been the case only because it could be exchanged at the United States Treasury for a gold dollar.   It was therefore not a difference in the current value of the two coins that caused the retirement of the gold money, but a fear in the public mind that the Treasury might at some time cease to redeem its silver money with gold. Nor was this fear by any means groundless. The Act of July 14, 1890, does indeed declare it as being "the established policy of the United States to maintain the two metals on a parity with each other," but this declaration is not sustained by the action of our government in the past, nor is it consistent with the spirit and letter of other portions of the act itself.

Bi-metallism has been the monetary policy of the United States from the beginning of the government, except for five years—from 1873 to 1878—during which time there was no metallic money in the circulation. At all other times, down to 1878, when the money of the country was on a metallic basis, it has been the policy of the government to let the two metals take their natural course, and this has invariably resulted in excluding from circulation the coin of higher bullion market value. The reason for this will be obvious when we reflect that, if in a transaction of trade the seller may exercise his choice, he will naturally demand the most valuable money obtainable, but if he must accept the money that is tendered to him, the buyer will pay him in that which has the least value. It is through such action by individuals, each prompted by his own interest, that bi-metallism operates to retain in the circulation the money of least value and to expel from it that of any higher value.

Nor can it be said to have been the policy of the government since 1878 to maintain the two metals at a parity, if we are to judge of that policy by the acts of Congress, and not by the practice of the Treasury department. The Act of February 28, 1878, commonly called the Bland Act, made no provision for maintaining the two metals at a parity; it simply authorized the injectment of silver money into the currency, and decreed that the silver dollar should be a legal tender at its nominal value. There is really no act of Congress which definitely commits the nation to maintaining the two metals at a parity, and it is the fact that the nation is not thus definitely committed that discredits our money. By making the two metals a legal tender at a fixed ratio, and thereafter abstaining from interference with the coin in circulation, which was the policy of our government down to 1878, the metal of higher value was expelled from the circulation, leaving the other metal to constitute the monetary standard. By thus permitting the metals to take their natural course, the United States, when on a metallic basis, had always had, down to 1878, a definite and stable money; in other words, the United States has theoretically had bi-metallism, but practically monometallism.

Since 1878, we have had bi-metallism in its most objectionable form, by reason of the effort made to force, by legislative decree, the circulation of the two metals at their nominal values, irrespective of their actual bullion values. This is what the Act of 1890 assumes to do in authorizing the Secretary of the Treasury to pay " in gold or silver coin *at his discretion*," since to maintain the two metals at their legal parity, it is absolutely necessary that the choice of the metal to be received shall rest with the recipient. This fundamental principle is now so generally understood and accepted that no intelligent person can be misled by an act which in one clause declares for the maintenance of " the two metals on a parity with each other," and in another authorizes the Secretary of the Treasury to pay in either metal at his discretion. In the exercise of this discretionary power the Secretaries have uniformly left the choice of the metals to the person receiving the money, and it is solely through this recognition of a monetary principle in their governance of the Treasury Department that the legal parity of the two metals has been maintained.

4

Congress can render no greater service to the nation than by substantiating its declared policy under a definite pledge to make the gold and silver money of the United States interchangeable at the Treasury at the option of the holder; nothing it can do would so quickly restore confidence and bring relief to an overburdened people. The repeal of the silver-purchase clause of the Act of 1890 was necessary and commendable; it relieved the country from a burdensome tax, but with our large volume of silver money, the remaining clauses of that act must continue to menace our credit so long as the nation is not definitely committed to redeem its silver money with gold.

We have now little cause to fear that the gold standard will not be maintained: in the agitation and discussion of the silver question, the people have come to realize the injustice that would be wrought by permitting the standard to drop from gold to silver, and on this moral ground, if not from the convincing force of economic logic, they will insist upon the maintenance of the gold standard. While we may ourselves be entirely confident that our government will honestly live up to its monetary professions, it is particularly unfortunate that any occasion should be given to other nations to question our good faith, and so long as the Act of 1890 remains in its present equivocal form, we cannot logically expect to secure or to retain foreign confidence ; but with a definite commitment of the nation to preserve the integrity of its monetary standard, all cause for distrust would be removed. We might then look forward with reasonable assurance to a return of the foreign capital that has been withdrawn from us, the loss of which is the chief cause of our industrial depression.

It is not money, but wise monetary legislation, that the country now needs.   There has been no time in the past two years, except during the few weeks when the " paper-money hoarding " craze prevailed, that the money in circulation, though wofully defective in quality, was not amply sufficient in volume for all demands; and if we include the hoarded gold money in the country, the volume has been greatly in excess of what could be profitably employed under normal conditions. It is admitted on all sides that a revision of our monetary system has become absolutely necessary ; but no revision can be of any service that does not re-establish public confidence in our money.

Before proceeding to illustrate the beginning and growth of paper-money, it may be well to con-

sider briefly some of the salient evils that would
result, in the event of a fall in our monetary standard
from the gold to a silver basis. If such a change of
standard were made with due consideration, the
government providing for the redemption in gold of
the silver money it had issued at a gold valuation,
and replacing it with silver money issued at its actual
valuation, and also requiring that all contracts and
obligations entered into during the continuance of
the gold standard should be settled on that basis,
the disturbance to industry would be only such as
must arise from the adjustment of values to the new
standard, and business would soon move along much
the same as if on a gold basis. Though our monetary standard would not be improved, no one could
then justly charge us with duplicity or bad faith;
but to let the standard drop from gold to silver
without making full provision for the change, would
be criminal neglect.

All metallic money should have a market value as
bullion equal to its current value as coin; if it has
not this, it is not true money, nor can it be the most
serviceable money. As our gold coin is worth as
much in bullion as in coin, it answers to this test ;
but our silver coin, if converted into bullion, would
yield only three-fifths of its current value, which

current value, as we have seen, is maintained only because a silver dollar can be exchanged for a gold dollar at the United States Treasury.

The bi-metallic ratio of the United States is sixteen grains of silver to one of gold. When this ratio was adopted it corresponded very nearly to the relative market values of the two metals; at present, however, one grain of gold will buy about twenty-seven grains of silver, which makes the bullion value of our silver dollar about sixty cents.[1] If, for example, we should melt five silver dollars and three gold dollars separately into bullion, the present market value of these two bits of bullion would be the same, and we should find this to be the case wherever sold.

As gold has been the standard in the United States since January, 1879, every dollar of silver money in the country, whether it be in coin or paper, has cost its owner a gold dollar, or the equivalent of a gold dollar; therefore a drop in the monetary standard to a silver basis would cause these owners to lose forty per cent. of their money. A person with five dollars of silver money in his pocket would lose two dollars; he would still have five dollars *nominally*, but *actually* only three, as the purchasing power of the five would

[1] This valuation is used throughout, to preserve uniformity in the calculations, though in Nov. 1893, when this was written, silver was worth less.

have shrunk to that of three.   It might seem to him
when he came to spend his five dollars that prices
had advanced, but what would really have taken
place would be a reduction in the value of his money
while it lay in his pocket.   Commodities, and property in general, would not be affected in value by
the change in the value of the money, as would be
evident to those who had gold money to spend.   In
the adjustment of values to the depreciated monetary standard, the advance in prices would disturb
for a time the prevailing idea of relative values; but
these changes in prices would be nominal ; values
would remain as they were, subject only to natural
fluctuations.

In the derangement of prices that would follow a
sudden change of the monetary standard, large
numbers of persons, not foreseeing the effect of the
change, would be likely in trading to underestimate
the value of their property in the new and cheaper
money, and thus they would sustain the full loss result-
ing from buying with gold and selling for silver.   The
better knowledge of monetary conditions possessed
by the few, and their larger opportunities for turning
this knowledge to pecuniary advantage, would enable
them not only to protect themselves, but to profit
by the ignorance or the limitations of their neigh-

bors; and thus much of the wealth of the country
would be aggregated in fewer hands.   But as values
of property in general would not be affected by the
depreciation in the value of the money, the direct
and immediate loss would inevitably fall upon the
owners of money, of bank-deposits, and of such
assets as were payable in money.   This loss would
fall mainly upon that great body of frugal and in-
dustrious working people that composes more than
half the population of the United States, as the
savings of these people are generally held in bank
deposits.   A large majority of them would not
understand the situation, and even if they did, it
would not be in the power of any considerable number of them to protect themselves.

The number of small depositors in the United
States cannot be less than eight millions; in a general
liquidation, these depositors would be found to be the
principal owners of the money that constitutes our
medium of exchange.   As their savings are usually
left quietly and permanently on deposit, this money
becomes, through the intricacies of exchanges in the
ordinary course of business, the active lendable money
of the nation.   The sum of deposits in savings banks
alone is $1,712,769,026.00, and the number of de-
positors is 4,781,605, making an average of $358.20 to

each depositor. As, however, but a small percentage of the money deposited in savings banks is allowed to lie idle, this money goes immediately back into circulation ; even the bulk of the reserve money of savings banks is held on deposit in commercial banks, which are the active distributors of money.

If the government should cease to redeem its silver money in gold, about a thousand million dollars of the circulating medium of the nation would drop to the silver basis ; but in order to ascertain the full percentage of individual loss on the depreciated money, we must take the total sum on deposit in the United States, and add to it the money in current use, as follows :

In commercial banks . . .	$2,967,248,529 00
In savings banks	1,712,769,026 00
In current use (estimated) .	500,000,000 00
	$5,180,017,555 00

Here we have a sum exceeding five thousand million dollars, upon which there would be a direct loss of forty per cent., or say two thousand million dollars.

While the change of monetary standard would not lessen the volume of actual capital in the country, the loss to individuals would be as abso-

lute as if their property had been annihilated
by fire; and nothing can be plainer than that the
great burden of this vast loss would have to be
sustained by the working people who had laid up a
little money in bank for safe-keeping, and for the
interest it would bring them. There would be no
levelling of fortunes, as is vaguely supposed by some
people, but only an increased disparity. Trades-
people, merchants, manufacturers, and the great
industrial corporations, have their capital invested in
goods and merchandise, in land, factories, and in the
products of factories: the value of all these would
be adjusted to the new standard without loss, and as
these industries are mainly carried on with borrowed
money, the loss from its depreciation would not fall
upon them. Nor would the banks that are the
lenders of money be the losers, for nearly all the
money lent by them belongs to their depositors;
banks would therefore in a large measure be able to
protect their stock-holders by keeping their reserve
money in gold.

A glance at the weekly statements of the National
Banks of the City of New York will show that the
gold held in reserve by them is really in excess of
their total capital.

CHAPTER III.

PAPER-MONEY AND BANKING.

WE have seen that the improvement in money as a medium of exchange began with the substitution of one commodity for another, because the incoming commodity was better adapted for the service required than the outgoing, and we have seen that silver and gold, having gradually established their superiority over all other commodities, became the only money of the civilized world. Since the adoption of these two metals, the improvement of money through displacement has proceeded very slowly. Silver being more plentiful than gold, and better adapted to the limited trade of early times, was the predominant money for many ages; but as trade developed into commerce, gold came more and more into use, and is now the chief money of all the more advanced commercial nations, while silver continues to be the chief money of nations second in advancement. This condition is in strict accord with the general march of development.

In the larger and more complex transactions of modern traffic, gold has two qualifications that render it superior to silver; these are, that very much less of gold than silver, in bulk and weight, is required to perform a given service, and that gold has more stability than silver and is therefore a more trustworthy measure of values.

Thus far, it may be noted that all the improvement in metallic money coming through natural displacement, seems to culminate in the supremacy of gold; but while this inference is probably correct, it is certain that improvement of money generally will not cease so long as trade and commerce continue. He deceives himself who believes that such constant improvement as we see around us, in all the implements and appliances of every department of industry, could be possible if the one instrumentality upon which all such advancement depends, and without which it would stop, had remained stationary. We may rest assured that money has continually improved in efficiency, except in places and at times when the industrial organism of society was disordered by warfare, or when arbitrary rulers interfered with the

natural order of progression. This view is supported
by the testimony of history.

While the question as to the superior serviceableness of silver or of gold was still unsettled, forces of
a more subtle character than those that had produced displacement, came into play to augment
indefinitely the monetary efficiency of these metals ;
these, in brief, were *intelligence* and *integrity*. It
may not be obvious at first sight that a people's
sense of what constitutes fair-dealing has anything
to do with the amount of metallic money needed by
them to conduct their business, but we shall see as
we extend our inquiry that as man rises in the moral
scale he requires relatively less and less of the money-
metals. Nothing more truly shows the degree of
civilization attained by a people than their estimate
of what constitutes right and wrong ; it is upon this
sense that *credit* must rest, and it is to *credit* that we
must look for the further growth and efficiency of
money.

Let us now see how this new element of credit became not only an indispensable quality of money,
but the only quality by which its efficiency could
be enhanced when improvement by natural displacement ceased. Take, for example, a community arrived at the silver and gold stage of monetary

advancement, but still hoarding all its idle money or hiding it in the ground for safe-keeping. This money would be used only by the owners of it, and as every transaction in trade would require a sum equal in value to the commodity exchanged, the volume of money employed, as compared with the volume of transactions, would be at its maximum.   From this stage, improvement would progress when the owners of idle money lent it to those who would put it to use.   This would be the beginning of *credit*, and the consideration paid by the borrower would be the beginning of *interest*.   Thus, by the introduction of credit—by lending instead of hoarding—the same money would be made to repeat its service indefinitely; the presence of the precious metals would still be required in every transaction, but by turning the money oftener, the volume of money employed, as compared with the volume of transactions, would be lessened, and the cost of maintaining the medium of exchange would thereby be cheapened.   To continue to hoard money and to supply the demands of growing trade by increasing the stock of precious metals, would not be monetary advancement; the burdens of trade would not be lightened in the least, and there would come a time when this slow and labored growth would be arrested by the mere physical inability of the people to handle the metals.

At this stage of development, it is only by the cultivation of intelligence and integrity that any monetary advance can be made; in trading with one another, men are impelled, by the incentive of profit, to exercise these higher qualities of their natures.   Through trade they are brought into closer relationship, and the distrust that led them to hoard their money, is gradually changed into confidence by the amenities of commercial inter-course.   With the lending and borrowing of money fairly established, there would soon arise the need of a middle-man to promote and facilitate these transactions; and the need would develop the *banker*. A competent, responsible, trustworthy person, hav-ing the confidence of the community, would find his services in demand ; he would become the depositary of lendable money ; practically, he would himself become the borrower from those who wished to lend, and the lender to those who wished to borrow.   His profit would be derived from charging a higher rate of interest than he paid ; when metallic money was deposited with him, he would give his receipt for it, and as he possessed the public confidence, his receipt would pass from hand to hand, performing the function of money with greater ease than could the metal itself. Here we have a second refinement of money through the agency of credit—the banker's receipt, as the beginning of paper-money.

It will be seen, and should be noted here, that the banker is himself an essential factor in the refinement of money through the agency of credit; to illustrate his importance in this respect, we will trace this development one step further before proceeding to consider paper-money. We may suppose that, through the stimulus to interchange developed by more efficient money, the trade of the community has so far increased as to require the services of several bankers to transact the business; and that when metallic money, receipted for by one banker, is lent by him, the borrower deposits it with another banker, who also gives his receipt for it, thus furnishing two receipts which circulate as, and perform the function of, money, though representing one and the same metallic base. Here we have a third refinement in the growth of money through the agency of credit.

In thus tracing the growth of money from improvement by natural displacement to improvement by credit, it has been with a view to greater brevity and a clearer outlining of principles that we have illustrated the process by a concrete example; but the delineation is drawn from actual history. Credit, as a factor in monetary improvement, opened a new era of industrial growth, which may be classified as only second in importance to the adoption of a medium of exchange.

History records that the goldsmiths of London were the first bankers and the first issuers of paper-money in that city.

The superiority of paper-money over metallic money consists: first, in its cheapness; second, in the readiness with which its volume may be expanded or contracted; and third, in the ease with which it may be handled and transferred. Beyond these three important qualifications, it has no monetary function that is not derived from the commodity in which it is redeemable. It may be issued against any property that has the qualifications to serve as a medium of exchange, but if the thing selected is deficient in any of the essential qualifications of money, the paper-money will be similarly deficient. For example, paper-money cannot be issued against land, for land itself has no adaptability for use as money. Mortgages on real estate, government, state, or railroad bonds, cannot perform the service of money, and therefore are unfitted to be a basis for paper-money.

As paper-money is but a "promise to pay on demand," the thing in which it is payable must itself have all the essential qualifications of money, and these qualifications, as we have seen, are possessed in the highest degree by silver and gold. It is these metals that perform all the essential duties of money; but by the introduction of paper, simply as their representative, the volume of money is increased and its efficiency enhanced.

To have a paper-money of high efficiency, two conditions are essential : it must rest upon its only true basis—the precious metals, and it must be bank, and not government, paper-money.

We saw that when our banker lent a portion of his metallic money, against which notes had been issued, it went to another banker, who also issued notes against it; but the fact must now be noted that when our banker lent the money, he received from the borrower an equivalent in value as security for its safe return ; consequently, although these notes exceeded in amount the metallic money against which they were issued, the security held fully insured their redemption. In the regular order of banking this is what always takes place; no paper-money issued by a bank ever finds its way into circulation until there is an equivalent in value deposited somewhere to secure its redemption.

The banker who issues paper-money is its natural guardian ; it is he who, impelled by the incentive of profit, assumes all the responsibility of its prompt redemption when presented for payment ; his property and his integrity are pledged to its redemption ; why then should the state interpose to relieve him from the responsibility of his own act ? Such interference can have no other effect than to lower the standard of banking integrity. The banker is the one man especially competent to judge of the character of the security that shall protect his notes while in circulation, and his interest lies in protecting them.

Bond-security as a basis for bank-notes is another example of false theory in our monetary legislation ; but the public mind has unfortunately become charged with the belief that such security is essential to a sound circulating medium, though no phase of the theory can be presented that will stand intelligent scrutiny. A bank is a dealer in money only ; if it should permit all its money to go into long-time securities, its banking capabilities would be exhausted ; if it is obliged to invest a portion of its capital in this way to secure its note-issue, its ability to serve its customers is crippled to that extent.

One important function of a bank is to gather up the idle money of its neighborhood and to keep it in active employment, and this is a bank's main source of profit. Exclusive of savings-banks deposits, the amount of money thus gathered and kept actively at work in the United States is almost three times as great as the total sum of the capital invested in the banking business. This money is generally subject to immediate call; a bank must be ready to pay the checks of its depositors whenever they are presented. It finds, however, that on the principle of general averages, it can lend the greater part of the money, and still meet all demands upon it; but in order to do so, it can lend on short time only, and it must have the right, if a loan be not paid when it becomes due, to sell the pledged securities of the defaulting debtor at his risk. These conditions may seem hard, but they are not of the banker's making —they are inherent in the business; a banker is of all men the least of a monopolist; he is much more the servant of his customers than their master. Indeed, banking is in a special sense a public business; a bank may be owned by only a few individuals, but the community where it is located has the larger interest in it, and the larger power over it as well. Most occupations may be conducted independently of each other, but this one is linked to all of them, and its prosperity is dependent upon their prosperity ; it is bound to them by ties of mutual interest.

When improvement in money through displacement ceased to meet the requirements of trade, the banker and his paper-money became a necessity ; the distrust which called for metallic money in every transaction had to give place to confidence, or trade could grow no faster than the volume of the precious metals increased. It is the confidence reposed in the banker that has created and that sustains his occupation ; for a bank cannot exist in an atmosphere of distrust. Through credit the banker gathers up idle money and keeps it employed ; through credit he issues his paper-money, which enables him to expand and contract the volume of money to meet the actual requirements of trade, and while profit is his prime incentive, his interest is also entirely in accord with legitimate trade and industry. It is to his intelligence and integrity that the world is indebted for the enhanced efficiency of money beyond the mere subdivision of the precious metals. But as the chief function of the banker in the industrial world is to facilitate exchanges, he does not fail to use such methods as tend to accomplish this with the greatest safety, in the shortest time, and with the least labor. Beginning with paper-money, he next introduces checks, every one of which effects an exchange more safely and speedily than any kind of money can ; more recently he has originated the clearing-house, which is another step in the same direction.

In the city of New York the daily transactions in trade are numbered by the millions, and ninety-four banks are required to make the exchanges. At the clearing-house on every business day these banks are represented by their accountants, and ninety-five per cent. of the business transactions of the previous day are settled, entirely by the exchange of checks and balancing of accounts, no other medium being used ; this clearing is accomplished in about an hour's time, the volume of business thus settled each day averaging one hundred and twelve million dollars.[1] The remaining five per cent. is settled with money, but it is mainly paper-money, coin being called for only when it is actually needed.

In estimating the growth of money in the world, it is impossible to ignore the services of the banker, for it is through his instrumentality that metallic money has been made to meet every legitimate demand upon it ; the industrial progress of the English-

[1] These figures give the average daily clearings for the year 1892.

speaking people for the past two hundred years has been largely dependent upon the banker's methods of monetary refinement. The mere recital of these methods should be sufficient to satisfy us that unless the banker is unduly restricted by legislative enactments, industry can never again languish for want of the means to effect exchanges. It may safely be said that the volume of business transactions throughout the world, now settled economically, securely, and speedily, through the agency of paper-money, checks, bills of exchange, banks, and clearing-houses, infinitely exceeds any volume that could be settled with metallic money alone, even if the earth were emptied of its precious metals and every ounce of them converted into coin. It would simply be a physical impossibility to transact this enormous business with the metals alone.

That the existing monetary methods adopted by the banker are the result of natural development is so obvious that the only wonder is that any intelligent person can be found to question it. Every step of this development lessens the volume of precious metals needed to transact a given amount of business; yet we must not infer from this that they can be dispensed with altogether; indeed, the need of them seems to be increased by the magnitude of the work they are made to perform. They are the standard of measurement in every transaction as much now as when they were the only money in use, and the mechanism whereby their usefulness has been so greatly enhanced revolves wholly upon the degree of certainty with which they can be had when actually needed and called for; it is thus that, by the logic of events, monetary growth has come to be dependent upon individual honesty. As metallic money is but a medium of exchange, every instrumentality whereby its work is accomplished becomes money in the larger sense, and as all these instrumentalities are bound by the inexorable law of equity, the only terms upon which industrial progress can be made, are exact dealing and strict adherence to the word of promise. Paper-money, the bank, the check, the bill of exchange, the clearing-house, all owe their existence to the observance of the principle of reciprocal justice between man and man; this whole fabric of credit, which has already produced such wonderful results, began with the individual, is of individual growth, and still clings to the personality of the individual.

It was the fundamental idea of the fathers in framing our Constitution that the people should retain, as far as possible and consistent with political unity, the management of their affairs ; that no power should be delegated to the county that could as well be exercised by the town ; that no power should be delegated to the State that could as well be exercised by the county ; and in like manner, that no power should be delegated to the federal government that could as well be exercised by the State. To make an application of this principle to the subject in hand—banking,—it may be stated that no power which can be exercised by a community should be delegated to the general government, and that banking is especially of such quality. All our monetary enactments since the issue of greenbacks, in 1862, have been in conflict with this principle. The Legal-Tender Act, the act taxing State-bank notes out of existence, the act closing the mints to free coinage of silver, and the act by which silver was mechanically injected into the currency, are all calculated to contract and obstruct the only avenue of monetary growth that is open to the people, and tend therefore to bring them into helpless subjection to the government at Washington. And these enactments are equally in conflict with the natural law of money, which is in perfect accord with, and promotive of, popular government.

It has already been said that government paper-money is not adaptable to the industrial needs of our country. In order to indicate with more exactness why this is so, and to show the superiority of a bank-note currency, it will be necessary for us to clearly demonstrate the importance of elasticity as a property of money. The volume of trade fluctuates widely, and even under normal conditions has seasons of activity and of dulness ; money should therefore be adaptable to these fluctuations. By the term " elasticity," when applied to money, is meant its responsiveness to trade demands ; it is said to have more or less elasticity in proportion to the ease and readiness with which its volume may be increased or diminished at a given point. Now, as the volume of metallic money cannot be readily expanded or contracted, its elasticity depends mainly upon the ease with which it may be moved from places where it is not needed to places where it *is* needed. On the other hand, paper-money—by which is meant bank-notes issued under a free system of banking—may be increased or diminished in volume at every point whence it is issued ; consequently its elasticity is not so dependent on freedom of circulation as that of metallic money is.

As will presently be shown, our government paper-money does not possess these elastic qualities, and as a natural consequence, the supply of money at all points of industrial production away from the commercial centres has been so uncertain as to produce a widespread unrest among our people. They realize fully the restrictions imposed upon their productive powers by this defective money, but they do not seem to understand that a government paper-money cannot be made adaptable to their local wants.

Bank-notes being credit-money, their circulation is necessarily limited to localities where they are known to be good, and if they wander beyond this range, they are sent home, even if their expenses have to be paid ; whereas, coin of full intrinsic value is returned only when there is a profit in returning it ; hence, paper-money is inherently local in character. All paper-money needs supervision ; it cannot be turned out-of-doors, as metallic money may be, without acquiring vagrant habits ; metallic money is self-constituted and self-sustaining ; it has established its status in every land ; but paper-money is as yet dependent and in a state of tutelage ; what its capabilities may become in the future, it is not now within our province to inquire ; as it has already out stripped all other money as a factor in wealth production, the important questions for us are: From what source does it derive its wonderful efficiency, and what are the terms upon which it will render its best service? In answering these questions, we shall find that the fact of its being local money is the basic reason for its efficiency, and that its terms for most effective service are that it shall work under the supervision of its issuer, whose interest is to keep it in productive employment.

Government paper-money, in the wide range of its circuit, acquires something of a nomadic character; it has no local attachments or home-ties; nobody indeed has any interest in it but its immediate possessor, and his interest ceases with the spending of it: bank-notes, on the other hand, will return frequently to their issuer to remind him of his obligations, and to keep alive the reality of their convertibility. When money is spent, the spender's interest in it ceases; but when it is lent, the lender's interest in it increases. Government money, when issued, is always spent money, no Treasury official having the least interest in it after it leaves his hands; whereas, money issued by a bank is invariably lent money, the banker's interest following it and keeping watch over the uses to which it is put.

The issuance of paper-money is properly a function of banking; the political mechanism of our government is not adaptable to banking, as the Treasury can pay out and take in money only through its regularly authorized expenditures and collections; it is powerless to adjust the volume of its money to the fluctuations of trade, hence we say government paper-money is deficient in elasticity; and the fact of its having a national circulation is another disqualification, so far as the industrial needs of the nation are concerned. In this vast country, government bills have but one point of issue, and that not an industrial, commercial, or financial one; they are sent off on their wanderings as *spent money*, and are soon caught up by the general drift that carries all such money into speculative dealings at the great financial centres. Nor could this money be made to serve industrial production with the efficiency of local bank-notes, even if a sub-Treasury with power of issue and redemption were planted in every town in the Union, because there would still be lacking that one supreme underlying motive power which turns all the wheels of industry—*the incentive of profit*.

Wherever paper-money has had a free individual growth, it will be found adapted to the occupations of those employing it: the banker's bill of exchange is the paper-money of international commerce, and the volume of transactions annually settled with this medium cannot be less than sixteen thousand million dollars; yet these monetary transactions proceed so quietly as to attract little attention beyond the circles immediately concerned in them. The bill of exchange is a free growth of individual credit; as its range of circuit is outside of national boundary lines, it has escaped the politician's meddling.

Nothing has done so much to obstruct the growth and improvement of paper-money in general, and to prejudice people against its use, as the making it a legal tender; this legislation was the means in colonial times of engendering for paper-money a distrust that still survives among the better educated people, while the common people are comparatively free from it. We may even now find among economic writers the opinion that the issuance of paper is wrong, notwithstanding the fact that they do not, and cannot, point out any possible means by which we can get along without it.

To explain this prejudice we must let the light of the colonists' experience with paper-money fall upon the facts of to-day. We shall see

that the shadow of the king's mandate rested
upon the colonies during the whole period from
the first issue of paper-money by the General Court
of Massachusetts in 1690, down to the day, in
1780, when, in sympathy with an aroused public
sense of justice, the Continental Congress by resolu-
tion begged the States to repeal their legal-tender
enactments, and to make an equitable settlement
with the holders of Continental bills. In view of
what was and what might have been, the story of
the struggles of the people of the colonies with
paper-money, looked at from an economic standpoint, becomes pathetic.   There was not, from first
to last, any proper conception of the real nature of
paper-money: that to give it stability, it must be
redeemable in coin on demand—that it is a growth
of individual credit—that it must have a local habi-
tation and personal supervision—had not yet entered
the minds of the most advanced monetary students ;
the people lived out their lives, generation after generation, in mental slavery to the idea that it was the
duty of the state to supply their medium of exchange.

   We need not recite the many fruitless attempts of
the colonists to produce an efficient paper-money ;
the story forms an interesting and instructive chapter in the history of our country.   Nothing is plainer

to the thoughtful reader who is looking for causes, than the fact that metallic money in the colonies became inadequate to the demands of their growing trade, and that this inadequacy created a condition which threw the balance of advantage into the scale of the money holder.   The time had indeed come for the people to use credit-money, but they did not understand its governing principles; they did not realize that the stability and efficiency of this kind of money are dependent upon public confidence, and that public confidence is simply an aggregation of the individual confidence; that individual confidence is a thing of spontaneous growth which can never be brought into being at sovereign command.   The colonists looked to the state as the only power that could supply their medium of exchange, and had not the least idea that it was to themselves they should look—that the state could do nothing to aid them beyond preventing fraud and certifying fact.

CHAPTER IV.

PAPER-MONEY IN COLONIAL TIMES.

THE paper-money, or bills of credit, of the different colonies varied more or less in minor details, but in its more important features it may be divided into two kinds: that which had only the guaranty of the colony for its redemption, and that which had in addition a real or personal security. As this latter money was the best ever issued by the colonists, and came to be held in special favor by them, we may confine ourselves to the consideration of this kind. It was put into circulation by the colony's lending it for a term of years on interest, and taking from the borrowers real or personal security; but as none of it was redeemable within a year of its issue, and much of it ran for five or for ten years, it could not maintain stability. The idea that paper-money could be made to maintain par value in circulation by redeeming it in coin on demand, seems not to have occurred to the colonists; they looked to the credit and authority of the state to impose this quality upon their money. The lack of public confidence in the money appeared to them to arise solely from a lack of confidence in its ultimate redemption; the thought evidently did not suggest itself to them that the most absolute certainty of remote redemption could not serve the bill-holder whose immediate necessities demanded metallic money, and that if there were but one such bill-holder among a hundred, the whole volume of paper-money would depreciate until his needs were satisfied.

The first issue of bills of credit was made by Massachusetts in 1690: it was not then known in England or in America why clipped coin should hold its place in the circulation, while coin of full weight could not; although this problem had been solved by Sir Thomas Gresham more than a hundred years before, its solution was not known to the colonists; it was therefore not to be expected that they should understand the workings of their paper-money. England, in common with monarchical Europe, had long before fallen into the way of looking at money as of the king's creation, and what England thought in reference to money, the colonists

thought. The crown arrogated to itself the power
to fix the value of money, and nobody questioned
that power. In the years following the introduction
of paper-money in the colonies, it came to be understood that metallic money was but a commodity
with which the people were as competent to supply
themselves as with any other commodity; but this
knowledge was confined to the few, and even the
few never understood the nature of paper-money.
Nor is there any evidence that the law of metallic
money was sufficiently assimilated by any one to
enable him to perceive that it was beyond the power
of the state to regulate the value of it, or that the
assumption of such power by the state was not one
of the legitimate prerogatives of sovereignty.

The repeated failures of the colonists to produce
a paper-money that would possess the stability of
coin, were attributed by them to the nature of the
money itself, and not to its inconvertibility; if they
had understood the governing principles they need
never have been without a sufficiency of good, serviceable money. The whole difficulty was that they
looked upon money as a thing that only the state
could supply, and they never freed themselves from
this mental delusion. The power they depended
upon to supply them was not only incompetent for

the task, but the coercive instrumentalities which it employed to force its defective money into circulation prevented the natural growth of credit-money which otherwise would have taken place.

Apparently there was always a sufficiency of metallic money in the colonies when it was not driven out by defective paper money ; but increasing trade, with its accompanying complexities, called for a more flexible currency, and the appearance of paper-money was in itself a proof that the time had come for its use. The amount of metallic money in the colonies just before the breaking out of the Revolution was estimated at from eight to twelve million dollars. (Alexander Hamilton's estimate was eight million.) The population of the colonies was then less than four millions. Canada, to-day, with a population of five millions, and a trade proportionately very much larger than that of the colonies, finds thirteen million dollars of gold (that metal being her only metallic standard) an ample basis for all her monetary transactions.

Within thirty years of the first issue of colonial paper-money it had come into general use in all the colonies, and in Massachusetts the demand for it was so urgent that it became necessary to establish county loan-offices in order that the borrowers might

have an even chance to obtain their *pro rata* share.
In the estimation of the wise and well-to-do of the
time, it was a " borrowing-passion," an " epidemic,"
that had gotten possession of the people. But even
a passion and an epidemic have their causes. Back
of this movement lay the imperative necessity, if
not for more money, at least for a more serviceable
money. The backwardness of monetary knowledge
at this time may be judged from the fact that, in
1722, George I. issued a patent to one William Wood
to make coin from pinchbeck for circulation in the
colonies.

Paper-money became a serious question in the
politics of the colonies, and continued to be so down
to the Revolution ; through the pressure of impersonal forces there was a constant demand for it
coming from the great body of the people. On the
other hand, it was deemed by many to be nothing
better than a corrupting monetary innovation. A
state wields no power so effective to lift or to lower
the morals of a people as its monetary legislation,
and no legislation could be more destructive of
morality than the paper-money laws of the colonists
—laws which put it into the power of a debtor to
evade the payment of his just debts, and thus per-
verted the sense of justice and offered a premium to

dishonesty ; laws which arbitrarily fixed the prices of commodities, irrespective of cost to the producer, thus striking down one of the chief incentives to industry and frugality, which is profit; laws which prohibited the exportation of coin and bullion, denying to the individual that protection which the state owes him to hold and use his property for his own benefit, and thus converts him into a smuggler and a contemner of law.

It is to this coercive and demoralizing legislation that the failure of colonial paper-money must be attributed, and not to the money itself, notwithstanding its defective character; its lack of stability and of elasticity would have had a tendency to misdirect industry and to incite to speculation, but if utterly vicious measures had not been adopted to force its circulation at a factitious value, we may fairly assume that it would have gradually grown in favor and that its quality would have improved by changes in the manner and form of issuing it. Although these arbitrary laws were not always in force, they were so frequently resorted to as to be inseparably associated with paper-money in the minds of the people. When coin was driven from circulation it was by the operation of the legal-tender quality given to paper-money, and not because the money was paper; but as this distinction never became clear to the popular mind, paper-money circulated under a cloud of distrust even during those times when it rested solely upon its intrinsic merits. Thus it was that the growth and improvement of colonial paper-money was stifled by the king's mandate.

In comparing the colonial paper-money movement with our silver movement, we find a marked similarity as well in the popularity of the two movements as in the character of the opposition to them. The colonist opponents of paper-money took the position that this money was a worse than useless innovation, and that their silver money was all-sufficient. This view was held as late as 1819, by John Adams, who was a student of monetary science; this is shown by the following extract from a letter of his of that year: " I am old enough to have seen a paper currency annihilated at a blow in Massachusetts in 1750, and a silver currency taking its place immediately, and supplying every necessity and every convenience." [1] The public demand for paper-money was attributed to personal dishonesty, and not to any need for this new money. In politics it became a question of individual morals rather than

[1] *Life and Works*, x., 375.

of finance, and there were examples of such rare integrity as men declining from principle to pay their debts in paper; yet the movement went on persistently at all times, when not suppressed by the home government, or when it had not, by excessive issues, broken down in utter wreck.   Notwithstanding all the difficulties attending the use of this money, it rendered considerable service to the colonists, and was generally admitted, even by its opponents, to have done excellent service during the revolutionary war.   Thomas Paine said of it: " Every stone in the bridge that has carried us over seems to have a claim upon our esteem.   But this was the corner-stone, and its usefulness cannot be forgotten." [1]

The paper-money movement of the colonists proceeded from the fact that they had reached the stage of industrial development when metallic money could no longer supply all their needs; and the common people's advocacy of the new money proved that their apparent ignorance was but the expression of a profounder instinct.   Our silver movement has an equally substantial warrant for its existence; it proceeds from the fact that the money that has been substituted for bank notes will not render ser-

[1] Letter to Abbé Reynal

vice where service is most needed ; the need of money
is felt, but the nature of the want is not understood.
It is believed to be caused by a scarcity of gold, and
that an increase in the volume of silver would com-
pensate for this deficiency and supply the need ; but
this view loses sight of the well-known historical
fact that two hundred years ago, when the magnitude and complexities of trade were relatively not a
hundredth part of what they are now, the English-
speaking people had reached the period of paper-
money, when without it the metals could no longer
supply their needs, and when further industrial
progress was only made possible by an intelligent
use of the new money.

The fact has been overlooked that since the
introduction of paper-money the natural trend
of improvement has been wholly towards an increase of credit-money, and a relative lessening
of the need for the precious metals. We have
been led away by the delusion that there is not
enough gold in the world to supply the world's needs,
ignoring the fact that it is *value* and not *volume* that
constitutes the money standard, and that, therefore,
stability is the essential point to be looked to. Under
the mistaken impression that the public craving for
money proceeds from insufficient supply and not

from defective quality, we have attached undue importance to the acts of foreign governments in demonetizing silver; yet while noting clearly the disturbing effects of their action upon the stability of silver, we have ourselves become the greatest disturbers of the silver market; by ignoring the fundamental monetary law which forbids interference with the free flow of the precious metals, we have for the time being rendered silver unfit for monetary use.

Because of the larger diffusion of intelligence and the larger trustfulness that is found here as compared with European countries, together with our immunity from sudden outbreaks of war, a very much smaller proportion of coin is needed by us than in the specie-paying countries of Europe. Indeed, ours is particularly a paper-money country. Notwithstanding the extraordinary effort made to force silver dollars into circulation by paying the express charges on them, the limit of possible output was reached at sixty millions, and these went mainly to the South, a fact that should be noted as showing how true it is that money will always find its way into the channels of employment for which it is best adapted. These dollars are eminently well-fitted to the simple trading of the negroes, and if we should adopt the single gold standard, excluding this coin from circulation, it would retard the industrial advancement of the South.   The negro prefers this money to either gold or paper.

Improvement in money proceeds altogether on practical lines, the impetus in that direction coming from the great body of the people, which concerns itself little with economic theories.   At the head of this movement is the banker, who has shown that when not trammelled by restrictive legislation, he is entirely competent to meet and provide for the varying conditions of trade that exist around him. But there has been no time in the history of our country when banking has not been more or less restricted by laws intended to protect the bill-holder and the depositor, which, while ineffective for the purpose designed, have operated to retard the growth of the business.

Considerable progress was made in banking methods in the interval between the Revolution and our civil war ; but the issuance of government paper-money as a war measure, together with the subsequent suppression of State-bank notes, revived the antiquated idea that it is the duty of government to provide the money of the people. It was this idea that retarded the growth of banking during the colonial period, and it is the prevalence

of the same idea to-day that is chiefly responsible for
our present monetary backwardness. This superstition so obscured the colonists' views in reference to
paper-money that they never got a glimpse of the
true principles of banking, and at no time did they
ever have a clear perception of money as simply a
medium of exchange. They continued to the end
to rely upon the authority and credit of the State
for their paper-money; this is evidenced by the fact
that, notwithstanding the ill-success of the individual
colonies with paper-money, it was the general belief
when the Continental bills were issued that this
" universal money," as it was called, being supported
by all the States, must certainly be a success. The
failure of Continental money finally produced a general disgust for all paper-money; the prejudice
against it was very strong and bitter, especially
among moneyed men and people of property; there
was still, however, a paper-money party in the country, though it was for the time quiescent.

This was the temper of the public mind in regard
to paper-money when the federal Constitution was
framed; specie was considered the only legitimate
money; the issuance of paper-money was held to be
a governmental prerogative, and the right of the
state to make it a legal tender was not questioned;

but in view of the evil effects already experienced, its issuance was regarded as justifiable only in cases of extreme emergency.

It was not until 1782, when the Bank of North America was started, that the first forward step was made towards the displacement of government paper-money by bank notes. These notes were payable in coin on demand, and were the first paper-money ever issued in America that recognized the essential principle of immediate redemption; but neither in America nor England was the potentiality of this principle fully realized. In neither country was it understood that in no way but through a faithful observance of the principle of immediate redemption could such a sense of public confidence be inspired as would maintain a paper currency at par. In both countries state support was deemed essential. The Bank of North America was practically a national institution; nearly two-thirds of its capital were subscribed by the general government, and it was absolutely under the control of the Finance Minister, Robert Morris. Its notes were receivable as specie for duties and taxes, and in payment of dues from the respective States.

The Bank of England, though at this time it had been in operation for eighty-six years, was still a government monopoly, overshadowing and obstructing any banking enterprise of an individual character. Its capital was government debt, against which notes were issued to an equal amount, and although these notes were payable in coin on demand, this principle, not being fully understood, was not carried out with sufficient promptness and uniformity to remove the distrust of paper-money that lingered in the public mind.

The Bank of England was undoubtedly America's model in banking, but the conditions in America were not such as to permit the establishment of a similar monopoly. The sensitiveness of the States in regard to centralizing power in the general government, combined with a deep-seated jealousy of monopolies, defeated the original design of the Bank of North America, which was to have been the fiscal agent of the nation, with a monopoly of bank-note issue. In this condition of public sentiment, the right of Congress to charter the bank was questioned; it was found that the Articles of Confederation contained no power to charter a bank; but as Congress had already pledged its word, and was itself depending on the bank to supply its pressing need of money, a compromise measure was adopted. The charter was granted " with a recommendation to the

States to give it all the necessary validity within their respective jurisdictions." It was also tacitly understood that the exclusive right of the bank to issue notes should end with the war. But the virtual admission by Congress of its defective powers, made it necessary for the bank to obtain a charter from the State of Pennsylvania, and the door was thus opened to joint-stock-company banking.

Before the present national government went into operation in 1789, New York and Massachusetts had each chartered a bank, and when the United States bank was chartered by the federal government in 1790, there were already in existence five corporate banks, holding State charters, with a capital of $3,135,000. In 1794 there were sixteen such banks; in 1796, twenty-four; and by 1804 there were sixty-five, with a total capital approaching $40,000,000.

Thus it was that through a fortuitous combination of circumstances, banking had broken away from the restraints of centralized authority, and was drifting on practical lines into its natural channel. By undertaking, in imitation of England, to issue paper-money through a national bank rather than directly by the government, a line of demarcation was drawn which finally left banking and the production of paper-money in the hands of the people. Though the

framers of the federal Constitution had practically
precluded the direct issue of paper-money by the
federal government, popular opinion in regard to
this form of money had not materially changed.   In
the public estimation, its issuance was a prerogative
of government ; but to transfer this power to a cor-
poration which, though absolutely under the control
of government, embodied in part individual ownership, was deemed to be incompatible with repub-
licanism.

The contest over the United States Bank which
in later years became a " burning question " in
national politics, had no reference to the prevailing
opinion that it was a function of government to
supply the people's money.   Hamilton, the founder
of the Federalist party, and Jefferson, the founder
of the Democratic party (then called the Republican
party), were at one on that point.   They differed as
to the expediency of issuing paper-money, Hamilton
favoring the issue and Jefferson opposing it ; though
both looked upon it as a fiscal agency rather than as
a medium of exchange.   Hamilton's preference was
for a single bank which, as the fiscal agent of the
general government, should be the only bank of issue
for the nation.   Jefferson was opposed to all banks
of issue, and a national bank he justly looked upon

as a centralizing agency in conflict with the principles of popular government.

A better understanding of the principles of money would have shown Jefferson how perfectly they harmonized with his theory of government; but he never clearly understood those principles, and the course that banking had taken disturbed him greatly in his later years. His failure to comprehend the personalism of money is the more remarkable because no one of the fathers of the republic had a truer sense of what constituted popular government than he; and no one of them was in closer sympathy with the great body of the people. The banking "mania" which had seized upon the people was unintelligible to him: "I believe it to be one of those cases where mercantile clamor will bear down reason until it is corrected by ruin," he wrote in 1813.[1] In 1815 he made the following peculiar statement in regard to bank-notes: "The banks were able for a while to keep this trash at par with metallic money, or rather *to depreciate the metal to a par with paper*, by keeping deposits of cash sufficient to exchange for such of their notes as they were called on to pay in cash."[2] In his plan

---

[1] Jefferson's *Works*, vol. vi., p. 232.
[2] *Ib.*, p. 434.

for reducing the circulating medium, submitted to
Mr. Rives in 1819, among other strictures upon the
issue of paper-money, he says : " Interdict forever
to both State and national governments the power
of establishing any paper bank " ; and again : " Certainly no nation ever before abandoned to the
avarice and jugglings of private individuals, to regulate, according to their own interest, the quantum of
circulating medium." [1]

And yet it is only through private individuals,
each acting in his own interest, that the quantum
of circulating medium can be regulated; if all monetary legislation were repealed, leaving the people
entirely free to produce their medium of exchange,
this medium could move only in one direction, and
that towards a higher degree of refinement.

Although the views entertained about money had
undergone but little change since colonial times, the
conditions stated, which had transferred the production and regulation of money from the general to
the State governments, brought this work closer to
the people and to their occupations ; it was not to
be expected that there would be any immediate
improvement of the monetary legislation of the
States over that of the general government, but with

[1] *Jefferson's Works*, vol. vi., p. 147.

7

thirteen distinct legislative bodies acting upon this one subject, there would necessarily be differences; these differences in course of time would demonstrate advantages, and this, taken together with their closer relations to the occupations of the people, would necessarily produce improvement in money.

It is not our purpose to follow the growth of paper-money under state legislation—much of this money was positively bad,—but before the breaking out of the civil war and the issuance of greenbacks, there were many instances where the money had reached a stage of development fully abreast with the best economic teachings of that time, and we need not doubt that, if the State banks had been permitted to continue the issuance of paper-money, we should by this time have a money as good as any nation has.

CHAPTER V.

THE MONETARY SYSTEM OF CANADA AS CONTRASTED WITH THAT OF THE UNITED STATES.

CANADA to-day, with a gold basis of about thirteen million dollars, supplies all her monetary needs with great efficiency; she is not only able to supply all her own legitimate wants, but has for many years rendered substantial aid to our western people in the movement of crops in the autumn; this was notably the case in regard to the heavy crops of 1891.

Canada's total authorized banking capital is something over seventy-five million dollars, and the paid-up capital a little less than sixty-two million dollars. The banks are permitted to issue notes equal to the amount of their unimpaired capital; the average circulation of bank-notes is about thirty-five million dollars, and the till-money is about fifteen million dollars, leaving twelve million dollars in reserve for extraordinary contingent demands. The demand for money during the harvest months is increased about twenty-five per cent., and the large bank-note reserve enables the banks to meet this special call for money without adding a fraction to the rate of interest; for when these notes are not in service, they are lying in the vaults of the banks without cost to the banks or to their customers.

There is no bond security for the bills; the only security is a first lien on the assets of the bank and on the double liability of the stockholders, the total amount of which security averages four or five times the total possible circulation, and seven times the average circulation. There is, besides, a note-redemption fund, contributed by the banks and held by the government for the immediate redemption of the notes of insolvent banks. This fund amounts to five per cent. of the total sum of notes in circulation during the previous year, each bank being required to keep its proportion good. The holder of a failed-bank bill has, besides, the guaranty of every solvent bank for the payment of his bill; the result is that every Canadian has a sense of complete security in the money of the country.

There has been no bank failure in Canada during the term of the present or of the preceding Banking Act (which latter dates from 1880), in which the assets of the insolvent bank were not sufficient to pay all the bill-holders. So far as can be ascertained, there has been no general suspension of specie payment in Canada within the past forty years; there was certainly no suspension there in 1857, when the banks of the United States suspended, nor has there been any since that time.

In submitting Canada's monetary system to the test of fundamental principles, the only defects we find are those which arise from legislative interference: her government has reserved to itself the right to issue legal-tender paper-money; the limit of such issue, as at present fixed by statute, is twenty million dollars, and of this total about nineteen million dollars has been put out. The government has also established a number of post-office and other savings-banks, competing with the corporate banks for the deposits of the people, thus crowding up the rate of interest upon the whole Dominion. As might be expected there is a bond security to the government paper-money. Gold being the only standard of value in Canada, this paper-money has for its basis of redemption fifteen per cent. in that metal, and for security ten per cent. in Dominion bonds guaranteed by the British government, and seventy-five per cent. in Dominion bonds not so guaranteed. The government retains to itself the issuance of all paper-money of a lower denomination than five dollars ; it also requires each bank to carry forty per cent. of its reserves in Dominion notes ; there are, however, no statutory restrictions on bank reserves, that matter being left very properly to the judgment of the banker. A reserve that is fixed by statute may operate as an embarrassment, but cannot as a security. Bank auditing, bank statements published monthly, a strict holding of the banks to their obligations under penalty of forfeiture of their charters, and, added to these, individual punishment for irregular or criminal banking, are the best securities the public can have, and these Canada has provided.

No better example can be found to illustrate the divergence in monetary ideas between the banker and the politician than is furnished by Canada. In all the essential characteristics of banking, the former is abreast with the intelligence of his time, while the latter still clings to the old notion that the State can arbitrarily enforce credit. By making the Dominion notes legal tender, and then compelling the banks to carry forty per cent. of their reserves in these notes, the Canadian government has needlessly burdened the banks, and in so doing has betrayed ignorance of monetary law. The same principles govern the relation between debtor and

creditor, whether a State or an individual is the
debtor; these principles operate with equal force in
either case, and cannot be set aside with impunity.

There is no such thing as compulsory credit; the
whole banking system of Canada rests upon a foundation of confidence; hence when the government
exacts from the banks an enforced credit of forty
per cent. of their reserves, it weakens this foundation, and with it the whole fabric of credit of the
Dominion.   But as the banks are amply able to meet
every legitimate demand upon them for coin, the
enforcing enactment is practically inoperative so far
as the people are concerned, since no judicious
banker would force these notes upon a customer
who needed coin; and it is to intelligent and upright
banking that Canada owes her great advantage in
the possession of an ample currency which is at once
safe, stable, and elastic.   The large measure of indi-
viduality and freedom conferred by the Banking'
Act of Canada has evidently been inspired by
bankers, as the government's own monetary methods,
if carried to their logical conclusion, are calculated
to undermine credit.

Canada's monetary system is a complete refutation
of the argument so persistently advanced among us
that there is not enough gold in the world to supply
the money needs.   The per-capita statisticians would

have us believe that we are helplessly dependent upon the volume of the precious metals for our medium
of exchange, and yet here is a country that main-
tains a paper circulation of $16.40 per head on a
metallic base of only $2.64 per head, without the
least strain to her credit[1]; while our paper-money
averages $16.40 per head with a metallic base of
$11.36 per head, $7.20 of which is silver and $4.16
gold.[2]   In computing this ratio of $11.36 to $16.40,

[1] The following figures, taken from the official statement of the
Canadian government for the month ending July 31, 1893, form the
basis, in regard to Canada, of these computations :

Authorized government note issue................	$20,000,000
Paid up banking capital against which notes may be issued...	61,954,773
Total note issue.............................	$81,954,773
Specie held by the government.................... .	$ 6,863,123
Specie held by the banks.........................	6,369,996
Total specie................................	$13,233,119

The population of Canada is computed at five millions.

[2] The following figures, taken from the official statement of the
United States Treasury for August 1, 1893, form the basis, in regard
to the United States, of these computations :

Silver certificates.............................		$333,031,504
Treasury notes................................		148,286,348
Greenbacks...................................		346,681,016
Gold certificates..............................		87,704,739
National-bank notes...........................		183,755,147
Total note issue...........		$1,099,458,754
Gold coin in Treasury	$103,363,626	
Gold bullion in Treasury...........	83,450,336	
Gold held by national banks........	91,764,347	278,578,309
Standard silver dollars in Treasury...	363,108,461	
Silver bullion in Treasury..........	119,277,735	482,386,196
Total specie...................		$760,964,505

silver is taken at its nominal value ; but as the object
is to show the very large proportion of metallic
money used by us as contrasted with the proportion
used by Canada, we must reduce our silver to its
gold basis of sixty cents to the dollar, in order to
make a uniform basis for comparison.   Our ratio
would then be $8.48 of metal to $16.40 of paper,
as contrasted with the Canadian ratio of $2.64 of
metal to $16.40 of paper.   In computing the amount
of metallic money in each country, only that is taken
into the account which is held by the government
and by the note-issuing banks of each country.

The fact that Canada's medium of exchange is
maintained at a proportionate cost of two-thirds less
than ours costs us, is evidence in itself that her monetary system is in advance of ours ; for, as has already
been shown, the trend of improvement in money is
now wholly towards the enlargement of credit and
the relative lessening of the use of the precious
metals.   As the proportion of metallic money to
credit-money is three times greater in the United
States than it is in Canada, this difference against us,
amounting to $378,673,350, may be regarded as just

The amount of gold held by the national banks is from the report
of the Comptroller of the Currency for the year ending October 31,
1893.

The population of the United States is estimated at sixty-seven
millions.

so much productive capital abstracted from industry
and converted into dead capital, for no one can doubt
our ability to maintain as large a proportion of credit-
money as Canada, if we will but adopt the proper
legislative measures. The abstraction of this large
sum from productive industry would be justified
if it contributed to enhance the efficiency of our
medium of exchange ; as it does nothing of the kind,
there is no way in which it can make the least return
to the people from whom it is taken.

As all our paper-money is either government or
national-bank money—and this latter is practically
a government issue,—it does not come into commercial use until it is weighted with its nominal
value in gold ; whereas sixty-eight per cent. of the
paper-money of Canada in commercial use represents
credit. In so far as the business interests of our
country are concerned, we have no credit-money,
and the only possible advantage derivable from the
use of paper-money is that it is more convenient
than the metals. Whatever profit accrues from the
issuance of paper-money, over and above the amount
of metal held for its redemption, goes to the government, and operates as a direct tax upon the medium
of exchange, and an indirect tax upon productive
industry. As no bank in the United States has,

aside from its deposits, a dollar of paper-money which has not cost a dollar in gold or its equivalent, it cannot afford to keep such money idle; whereas, out of the total issue of eighty-two million dollars of paper-money in Canada, the banks hold about fifty-six million dollars, which represent credit, and which they can issue to their customers as required, or can carry in their vaults without cost to either bank or customer.

A comparison of the practical working of the two banking systems, as applied to agricultural industry, will illustrate more clearly the superiority of the Canadian system. Our western farmers and southern planters, as a rule, have not sufficient capital to carry on their work throughout an entire year without aid; they are consequently dependent for supplies between spring and autumn upon the local storekeeper and the local banker. Few of them indeed can get through the winter without using their credit; but when autumn comes and they have marketed their crops, there is an all-round settling of accounts. This necessarily calls for a much larger amount of money in the autumn than is required at any other time of year. As these conditions are fixed by the seasons, it becomes necessary that all business dependent upon or accessory to agriculture shall be made adaptable to it. The country store-keeper, recognizing this fact, brings his business into conformity with it, and so does the local banker, as far as he can ; but as he cannot exercise his functions with the same freedom as the store-keeper or the Canadian banker can, his ability to serve his customers is greatly curtailed. The Canadian banker makes his own paper-money, which, though in the form of bank-notes, because of their greater convenience, is nothing more than checks upon his own bank ; *our* local banker is compelled to get his money from the national government, and pay therefor its full denominational value in gold ; and this is the case whether his bank is national or state.

The effect of this difference is that it costs the Canadian banker little or nothing to keep an ample supply of money on hand awaiting the contingent needs of his customers, while it costs our banker the full average rate of interest on the money so held ; he is therefore obliged to keep his lendable money constantly employed in order to make it pay. Hence, when the demand for money is light at home, he sends his surplus to his corresponding bank say in Chicago or New York, where he is allowed interest upon it at a rate of a third to a half the average prevailing rate. Thus it is that the money of the interior drifts to the great commercial cities, where it can always find employment in speculative ventures, if not in legitimate commerce.   A million bushels of wheat transferred speculatively ten times will lock up in margins as much money as the wheat is worth ; and when these transactions are all liquidated, the result in wealth production to the nation at large is *nil.*

But it is not necessary to own wheat in order to sell it speculatively ; all that is needed is money.   It would tax the ingenuity of man to make a money less fitted for industrial purposes and more easily drawn into these whirlpools of unwholesome specula-tion than our government money is.   A money that has no local ties, no specific qualifications for definite work, but that is a " Jack of all trades," will always elude supervision ; and all paper-money, to be indus-trially productive, must have personal supervision. But as this implies an acquaintance with the workers and a knowledge of their work, the area of super-vision is naturally circumscribed by individual limita-tions.   While the bankers of the great cities where this money accumulates may, from their more com-manding position, have a larger general knowledge of the monetary needs of the country than the in-terior banker can have, in the essential details of

lending money they are equally confined to their
own field of supervision. What, for example, can a
New York banker know of the qualities of the local
commercial paper and collateral that is brought to
him for re-discount by a Georgia banker? Practically nothing ; he has to take the word of the Georgia
banker, and however highly he may estimate that
word, his mind is still impressed with the difference
between a loan made at home upon his own judgment and knowledge, and one made at a distance
upon the judgment of another ; and this risk, whether
real or imaginary, not only limits the disposition to
lend, but raises the rate of interest charged.

The centralizing tendency of our money operates
as another disadvantage to the rural banker by reducing his deposit account (a chief source of profit
to the metropolitan banker), thus leaving the former
mainly dependent for his profits upon the rate of
interest charged. Hence we find that the Dakota
farmer pays two to three per cent. per month for the
money he borrows, while the Manitoba farmer pays
three-quarters of one per cent. Notwithstanding the
fact that our banks have relatively more capital than
the Canadian banks have, they are not able to fully
meet the legitimate demands made upon them.
Dotted all over the West and the South are these in-

dustrial banks at local centres, with veritable capital
and under excellent management, which are yet unable to supply money that they would gladly lend if
they could. Yet in the eastern States there is a preva-
lent belief that the call for more money which comes
from the West and the South, comes only from those
who have nothing to give in return for it; for it is
said : " As money is always seeking a level, by flowing
from points where it is in excess to points where it
is in demand and can find safe employment at higher
rates of interest, any one in good credit, or who has
the proper security to offer, can always borrow what
he needs." Under a natural monetary system this
would be so, but under our present artificial system
it is not so. What better collateral security can
there be than the products of the farm and of the
plantation, and who more competent than the local
banker to judge of the character of such security?
Give him the same freedom as the local store-keeper,
and he will serve his customers with the same thor-
oughness; it will not then be a question with the
farmer as to how he shall get money to carry on his
legitimate undertakings, but there will be a competition among bankers to serve him.

The situation in Canada to-day is that every legitimate demand for money is supplied.   To be assured

of this fact it is not necessary for us to know the details of the actual transactions, for conclusive evidence is furnished in the published statements of the banks, which show that they have at all times a surplus of bank-notes in their vaults awaiting employment. While money is just as available at one point of the Dominion as at another, the rate of interest, although not the same at all points, is uniformly steady, and the difference in rate between one point and another is due to the difference in cost of conducting banking at different points. The merchants of Winnipeg borrow money at about the same rate of interest as is paid by the merchants and manufacturers of Montreal, the financial centre; and the farmers of the far West pay about the same rate that is paid by the farmers of Ontario. The importance of an ample supply of money and a stable rate of interest, in encouraging and aiding industrial productiveness, can hardly be over-estimated; for obviously no intelligent person will risk his credit and property in industrial operations that cannot possibly yield him any return within a year, unless he can know beforehand where he is to get his money and how much he is to pay for it.

But how can any one know anything about the future of *our* money? It may have the intrinsic

value of gold to-day, and before the year expires be
down to the price of silver; it may be abundant at
six per cent. per annum when a business operation
is undertaken, and be scarce at thirty-six per cent.
before it is closed. These are the conditions that
environ the workers, the wealth-producers of the
United States, and they are the result of the government's undertaking to be banker-in-chief for the
nation. The demoralizing tendency of such conditions, which stimulate speculative ventures and dis-
courage legitimate industry, needs not be pointed
out. Nor need we be surprised that the farmers and
planters are impressed with the belief that there is
a moneyed conspiracy against them. In the interest
of the whole country, is it not well that there should
be a "greenback craze," a "silver delusion," and a
continued agitation, until the most productive of all
our industries is relieved from the incubus of a false
monetary system, since these are the surest signs
that there is an evil that needs correction?

If any more evidence is needed to prove the inability of our local banks to perform their proper
functions, we have it in the fact that our western
grain dealers are obliged to resort to Canadian banks
for monetary aid. It is estimated that in the autumn
of 1891 more than three million dollars were bor-

8

rowed from these banks for use in Minnesota and
Dakota alone.   It may be said that the grain-dealers
resort to the Canadian banks only because they can
borrow at a lower rate of interest ; but is not this of
itself a full concession of our contention that our
local banks are unable to perform their functions?
It is solely because they are deprived of the right to
issue their own notes on the security of the grain, as
the Canadian banks do, that they are unable to com-
pete with these banks.   On what better security
could paper-money be issued than on a bill of lading,
or a warehouse receipt with accompanying insurance
policy, which is the collateral given by the grain-
dealer ?   The Canadian banks do not send gold into
the United States to perform these services ;   they
are able to come to our aid simply because their implement for effecting exchanges is of higher refinement than ours, and it is so by reason of its having
less gold in its composition and more intelligence
and integrity.

The idea which prevails among us that in some
exceptional sense Canada is backed up by British
capital, ignores the established principle that
capital is not limited by nationality.   The motives
that move English capital are a sense of security
and a higher rate of interest or of profit than

can be realized at home, and it will come to the
United States on these terms just as readily as it
will go to Canada.   It was reported last July (1893)
that Canadians "loaded with English capital" had
appeared at Duluth as buyers of grain, when prices
had broken in consequence of the hoarding of our
currency.   Now, we venture the assertion that if, as
stated, Canadians went to Duluth to buy grain, they
employed neither English capital nor English credit.
A sight draft of the Bank of Montreal on its representative in New York for the purchase money would
be a satisfactory form of payment to the seller of
the grain; we may suppose the grain then shipped
via the Lakes and St. Lawrence River to Liverpool,
where it would be immediately convertible into
English money; the bank meantime being in secure
possession of the grain by bill of lading.   But the
bank could realize upon the grain before it arrived
in Liverpool; it could authorize its agent in New
York to draw a sixty-days' bill of exchange on its
agent in London, and this it could convert immediately into cash in New York, even in time to pay
the draft from Duluth.   It will be seen that the only
capital that appears in this transaction is the grain
itself, the credit of the Bank of Montreal being the
medium of exchange.

CHAPTER VI.

MONEY, CAPITAL, AND INEREST.

MONEY is not capital, nor is capital money, though these words are often, in common parlance, used interchangeably ; but there is a marked difference in their signification which should not be lost sight of. Strictly speaking, money is never anything but the common medium of exchange, whereas capital is an investment, producing some income. The term capital is commonly applied to the kind of investment known as personal property, such as the bonds or stock of railroads, or the capital stock of a business, which may include the money in use at the time and the building in which the business is conducted ; but the name is not applied to land, nor to real estate, nor to money in general, though it may be applied to metallic money. When we speak of a capitalist, the idea conveyed is not merely of a man of wealth, but of one who has his wealth so at command that it is readily convertible into money,

or into other forms of wealth through the agency of
money. It is doubtless because of the intimate
relationship between capital and money, and the
mobility of both, that the words overlap occasionally,
even when their significance is understood; but the
distinction between them becomes important when we
inquire into the real purport and function of money.

Let us suppose that A has capital in England
which he finds he can invest more profitably in the
United States, and so concludes to transfer it from
England to this country. It is stock in a brewery,
paying him six per cent. per annum, and he finds he
can make a similar investment here that will pay
him nine per cent., so he sells his English stock, receiving English money therefor; with this money he
buys a bill of exchange on New York, and with the
American money received upon it here he pays for
the American brewery stock. In this example, no
English money passes from England to the United
States—the thing transferred is capital. The English money which bought the bill of exchange remains in England, and the American money which
paid for the American brewery stock remains in
America, and goes immediately back into circulation
to continue the performance of similar services: this
is all that money ever does.

If, instead of a bill of exchange, gold had been sent to America, it would have been a transfer of capital. Bills of exchange, though not money in the strict sense, may not inappropriately be termed the paper-money of international commerce, as they perform in commercial dealings between different countries precisely the kind of service that paper-money performs for people of one country. Drawn mainly against exports of commodities which thereby become security for the payment of these Bills in gold (that metal being now the common measure of value in international commerce) they economize the use of gold, reducing the amount to one or two per cent. of what would otherwise be required.

There is a limit to the amount of money that may be used productively, but there is no limit to the amount of capital that may be used productively; the use of money is limited by the number of transfers to be made; the use of capital has no limit short of the exhaustion of nature's productive resources—which is practically no limit.

In the old world a vast amount of floating capital has accumulated from past ages; but in the United States the supply of capital is insufficient for the employment of all our labor and the development of our immense natural resources; the effect of these conditions is to make the normal rate of interest much higher with us than it is in Europe. In lending money, the rate of interest is influenced, first, by the degree of safety with which the loan may be made, and secondly, by the scarcity or abundance of money at the time the loan is made; but underlying these two changing conditions is the relative proportion of capital to opportunities for profitable investment of capital, which is the governing condition in fixing what may appropriately be termed the *normal* rate of interest; this normal rate is the more permanent rate which appears in first-class long-time loans. These three factors—the sense of safety, the supply of money as proportioned to the need for money, and the supply of capital as proportioned to the need for capital—dominate and govern the rate of interest.

All attempts to regulate interest artificially by legislative enactments which ignore these natural conditions, are but interferences which tend to lower the standard of business integrity, to advance and make unsteady the rate of interest, and to limit productiveness.

Every one knows that the rate of interest is affected by a sense of safety or of distrust on the part of the lenders and investors of money;

but that it is differently affected by money and by capital is not so generally realized. Indeed, much of the confusion of thought in regard to money and interest arises from the want of a clear perception of the differing functions of money and of capital. It is a very common mistake to suppose that more money is needed where it is really capital that is needed. All peoples have it in their power to supply themselves amply with a money of such efficiency as is best adapted to the stage of their industrial development; but the same cannot be said of capital, for capital is wealth, and the accumulation of wealth is a slow process even in a country as rich in natural resources as ours. On the other hand, money, as now constituted, may be nine-tenths *credit*, and all that is required of a people in order to have an ample supply of efficient money is an intelligent recognition of this fact, and the formulation of its monetary laws in accordance with it.

Now let us apply these principles to the question of interest. If we may assume all transactions in money to be equal in point of safety, it may be stated as a general principle that the more permanent or normal rate of interest is regulated by the volume of capital, and that its temporary fluctuations are produced by abnormal fluctuations in the volume of money: if the quantity of money in circulation is less than is actually needed, the rate of interest will be above the normal level; if it is more than is needed, the rate will be below.   Hence it follows as a corollary that if a people can keep the volume of its money just equal to the needs, the rate of interest will be just equal to the normal rate.   Hence it follows also that temporary and violent fluctuations in the rate of interest, which are so common with us and so disturbing to individual enterprise, would not occur if the volume of money were self-regulative, as it would be if the supplying of the money were left, as is the supplying of commodities, entirely to individual action.

If we may now assume the disturbances to interest, proceeding from abnormal fluctuations in the volume of money, to be eliminated, the rate of interest will then be affected only by capital, and will be a steady, though not a stationary rate; it will fall with the increase of capital and rise with its decrease; but as changes in the volume of capital take place slowly, changes in the rate of interest will be correspondingly slow.   The rate of interest will not be the same in all parts of the country, because the proportion of capital to profitable investment of capital, is not the same everywhere;

but as the movement of capital is always from points of less profit to points of greater profit and equal safety, there is a general and constant tendency towards an equalization of the rate of interest; and as in our country there is a constant accretion of capital, the natural tendency of the rate of interest is downward.

Another point to be considered in this connection is that there is a fixed relation between the volume of capital and the volume of money: where there is much capital, more money will be needed than where there is little, for the number of transactions will be greater, and the volume of money must be exactly sufficient to accomplish all the exchanges required, or productiveness will be diminished; additional money without additional capital can add nothing to wealth production.

As an illustration, let us take the fixed property of a railroad as analogous to capital, and its rolling-stock as analogous to money. It will be readily seen that when the number of cars is exactly equal to the traffic, the earning power of the road, in so far as it is dependent upon car equipment, is at its maximum. Similarly, when money is exactly equal to the exchanges to be made, the earning power of capital, in so far as it is dependent upon money, is

at its maximum.   What would be thought of a railroad company that should increase its car equipment beyond the possible requirements of its traffic?
Yet this is precisely the character of our work in
enlarging the volume of money regardless of capital;
nay more, to further this purpose we have abstracted
an immense amount of capital from productive industry, thus at one stroke increasing the volume of
money and lessening the possible need for it; by so
doing we have placed ourselves in the position of a
railway company that sells a portion of its road-bed
in order to buy an excess of rolling-stock.

By making a money of doubtful stability, we
drive capital away from our country, because with
an indefinite measure of values it is impossible for
foreign capitalists to calculate the outcome of their
investments here.   If Congress should enact that
twenty inches shall be the equivalent of thirty-six
inches, so that measurements made by a yard-stick
of either length would be an equivalent legal tender,
such an act would be no more absurd than the
monetary law which declares a silver dollar to be the
equivalent in value of a gold dollar.   Definite standards of weights and measures are absolutely essential to trade and commerce, and a definite money-
measure is equally so.

Within the twenty years following the close of our civil war we had a remarkable example of the beneficial effects produced by the introduction of foreign capital into a country. Our government having established its power to maintain itself, had inspired the world with confidence in us, and this confidence was reinforced and our credit greatly strengthened by the Act of January 14, 1875, which authorized the resumption of specie payment on January 1, 1879. Capital began to come to us soon after peace was restored, but after the passage of the Resumption Act an increasing inflow gave decided impetus to all our industries; this was more especially manifested by the yearly increase in railway mileage. The number of miles of railway built in 1875 was seventeen hundred and eleven, which was nearly doubled in the following year, and in the year appointed for resumption there were built four thousand seven hundred and forty-six miles, while in 1882, the increase in construction had risen to eleven thousand five hundred and sixty-eight miles. Resumption had actually taken place in 1878; the mere announcement of our intention to put our money on a sound metallic basis had brought capital to us in such abundance that resumption was not only made easy, but the normal rate of interest was reduced. The normal rate in the city of New York, which had formerly been six per cent. per annum, dropped to four per cent., and a corresponding decline took place in other parts of the country. This remarkable reduction in the rate of interest occurred within a space of two or three years, and is explainable only on the ground of a large influx of foreign capital, as it was not possible for us to have created in so short a time sufficient new capital to produce so great a change.

The year of actual resumption (1878) was also the year in which we entered upon that anomalous silver legislation, which has since so greatly disturbed the confidence inspired by the Act of Resumption; but as in that year the market value of silver was not much below our legal ratio, and as the decline that had taken place was supposed to be temporary, being attributed mainly to the action of Germany in demonetizing silver in 1871, the evil effect of that legislation was not immediately felt. Not until it became apparent that silver was declining from increasing production, as well as from demonetization, was confidence at all disturbed, and even then no serious apprehension was felt, because as yet nothing had occurred in the history of the United States to justify the least fear in any mind that our government would permit a law to continue in force which endangered the stability of its money.

In view of the discredit into which our country has recently been brought by mistaken legislation in reference to silver, it is of the first importance that every American should understand and appreciate that the United States, from its beginning as a nation down to the present silver legislation, has held a record for monetary integrity not surpassed by that of any nation in the world. In the founding of the Republic and in the framing of the Federal Constitution, there was no subject that received more solicitous consideration than that of making our measure of values honest and stable. Impoverished as the country was at that time by the drain of a long war, no hint of compromising this principle was ever uttered in the national councils ; and as the foundation was laid, so the superstructure was built.

When in 1834 the legal ratio of silver and gold was changed from fifteen to one to sixteen to one, the object was to restore gold to the circulation, as it was undervalued in the first ratio and had been practically out of circulation since 1792. Although under the ratio of sixteen to one the difference in the market value of the two metals was but slight, this difference had nevertheless the effect of displacing the undervalued metal, which in this case was silver. There is but one way in which the two metals can be held in circulation at a parity under any ratio that may be adopted, and that is to close the mints to the free coinage of the cheaper metal and make it redeemable in the other. In referring again to this phase of our subject, our object is to call attention to the fact that in changing the legal ratio of the precious metals in 1834, due regard was paid to preserving the stability of the national money. Although in adjusting the ratio (which is always difficult to do with values that are never stationary), silver went out of circulation and gold came in, the change was so gradual that it did not sensibly affect the monetary standard.

Clearness of definition as to the measure of values has characterized the monetary legislation of the United States down to the time that the silver question made its appearance in politics. Even the civil-war period of specie suspension cannot be regarded as an exception to this rule; the issuance of the greenbacks did not demonstrate that the national sense of honesty was growing weak, for there was no indefiniteness in the legislation that put that money into circulation; the terms of redemption were plainly stated on the bills themselves, so that the holder was just as competent to judge of their character and value as was the government that issued them. Nobody had occasion to ask, as is now asked about our silver money: What is the purpose of the government in reference to it? Immediate redemption was not then deemed possible, but all means were used that were practicable under the stress of civil war to make a stable money. It was made exchangeable for government bonds paying six per cent. interest in coin, and this feature of the Act of 1862 testifies to the honesty of its framers, and to their intelligent solicitude that the money should remain in circulation no longer than the exigency required.   Their mistake was in making the greenbacks a legal tender, though they doubtless believed, as we do not, that this feature would contribute to promote the stability of the money.

In order properly to compare the Greenback Act of 1862 with our late silver legislation, we must keep distinctly in mind that the act was passed as a means of raising money to meet the extraordinary expenditures of the war.   There was no pretence of making a better money than we already had ; it was in fact a borrowing act, and was not regarded by its authors as in any true sense a monetary act, nor was there any misunderstanding at home or abroad as to its character in that respect. Nevertheless this act was the beginning and the source of the monetary delusions that subsequently took possession of the public mind—delusions which gave us a Greenback Party, followed in turn by a Silver Party; but for this misdirection of the public thought, the framers of the act cannot be held responsible; they realized fully the imperfect character of the money they were issuing, and in making it exchangeable for government bonds they did the best that could be done to secure its retirement from circulation so soon as the people should be able to replace it by a more stable and efficient money. That it was a serious mistake to make the greenbacks a legal tender, we need not doubt, for it could have no other effect than to lower the credit of the United States, and to prompt the withdrawal of capital from the country. We may well believe that if the money had rested solely on the credit of the nation, it would not have declined to thirty-five cents on the dollar, as it did in July, 1864. The issuance of mandatory money is in its essence a declaration of bankruptcy; how then can it strengthen the borrowing power of a state?

9

CHAPTER VII.

MANDATORY MONEY AND FREE MONEY.

THERE is no reason to doubt that it was the
intention of the framers of the Constitution
to withhold from Congress the power of making
paper-money a legal tender ; but in order to appreciate properly their attitude on this point, we must
try to look upon money through their eyes. They
had not the remotest idea that their country had
entered upon a stage of civilization that made the
use of paper-money imperative ; it was therefore not
with any thought of supplying the people with a
paper-currency that the question was discussed in
the convention that framed the Federal Constitution. It was the borrowing clause of the Constitution that elicited debate ; there was but little
difference of opinion as to the adjustment of the
money clauses ; the coinage and the general regulation of money were reserved to Congress, and the

States were prohibited from making anything but gold and silver a tender in payment of debts.

In the opinion of the Fathers of the Republic coin was the only money that the people needed; paper was but an incident, a make-shift that might be used to bridge over periods of scarcity of coin; it was in no sense regarded as a permanent medium of exchange. It was chiefly as a ready means of raising funds for the State in emergencies that the question of paper-money was discussed by the members of the Convention, and we must look at it from their standpoint if we would understand their action. They doubtless considered it the duty of government to supply the money and to regulate its value; had a paper circulation been contemplated, discussion upon this point, followed by the embodiment in the Constitution of specific rules for its regulation, would have been inevitable. What they discussed was paper-money as a fiscal expedient; they had already had experience of paper-money, and they were not only greatly impressed by the injustice it wrought to individuals, but had also become convinced that it closed more avenues of financial resource than it opened.

Upon these grounds alone, they withheld from Congress the right to issue paper-money, for it was that right that was stricken from the Constitution,—paper-money as they understood it, not as we understand it. To them "bills of credit" and "paper-money" were synonymous terms which represented what is known to us as non-convertible legal-tender paper, and the mandatory character of this money was so identified in the public mind with these terms that it was not considered safe to let the harmless word *bills* stand, lest it might suggest and lead to an issuance of such money. Madison's suggestion that it might be "sufficient to prohibit the making the bills a tender" received no support; another member declared he "had rather reject the whole plan [of the Constitution] than to retain the three words *and emit bills*." The exercise of the mandatory power was deemed necessary to regulate the value of the money, whether paper or metallic; this was the political doctrine of that age, accepted by every government in Europe. The opposition to the striking out of the words "and emit bills," which gave rise to the debate in the Convention, proceeded from a reluctance to deprive the new government of the exercise of a power which was recognized by all as a legitimate attribute of sovereignty; as it was expressed by Mr. Randolph, notwithstanding his antipathy to paper-money, he "could not agree to strike out the words, as he could not foresee all the occasions that might arise " for the exercise of that power.   Antipathy to paper-money was the controlling sentiment of the Convention, moved as the members were by the injustice it had wrought; if they had seen that its legal-tender quality was the poison that produced these evil effects, it is likely that Mr. Madison's proposition to retain the word *bills*, but prohibit the making them a tender, would have met with approval.   In view of the fact that in their day the right of a state to issue mandatory paper-money was not questioned, no act of the Fathers of the Republic marks more decisively their high standard of political virtue than the withholding from Congress the right to issue such money.

The erroneous belief that it is a duty of the State to regulate the value of money is the parent of all the vicious monetary legislation in the world; born of an old superstition that a mysterious power of sovereignty imparted to coin an added value, it has obstructed the growth of money at every stage of advancement.   In the effort to construct a single money - standard from two independent money-metals, the law of natural displacement is ignored, and the failure to produce the result aimed at, leads logically to the expulsion of one metal from monetary use, and thus disturbs in both the element of stability which is so essential.   Bi-metallism, monometallism, fiat money, and the notion that the supplying of money is a function of government, are all the logical outcome of the false premise that the State can impart value to money.   That this delusive doctrine should have been accepted in an age when it was believed that the king's touch would cure disease, is not remarkable ; but that it should have a host of supporters in this age of steam, of electricity, and of practical common-sense, is strange indeed.   Why we of the United States, who deny that divinity doth hedge a king, and who aim to restore sovereignty to its true source—the people,— should still cherish this worn shred of monarchical prerogative which has no possible application of usefulness, is difficult to explain.

No government has ever yet succeeded in holding silver and gold at any fixed ratio of value ; the efforts made to accomplish this object have only tended to disturb natural relative values, to impair the efficiency of money, and to retard industrial progress. A fiat monetary law, whether applied to the metals or to paper, is not in harmony with the genius of our government, but belongs to the past, when govern-

ment was *rule*. " The laws of a country ought to
be the standard of equity, and calculated to impress
on the minds of the people the moral as well as the
legal obligation of political justice.   But tender-laws
of any kind operate to destroy morality and to
dissolve by the pretence of law what ought to be
the principle of law to support—reciprocal justice
between man and man." [1]   There is no more use for
a special law to compel the receiving of money than
there is for one to compel the receiving of wheat or
of cotton.   The common law is as adequate for the
enforcement of contracts in the one case as in the
other; nor from the transactions of trade and commerce can one be cited where a legal-tender law is
of the least utility.   It holds its place simply from
habit and custom—a custom that would be more
honored in the breach than the observance.

It must be admitted that, at first sight, the idea
of having one monetary standard rather than two is
beguiling, but a little consideration will show that
this idea proceeds directly from the monarchical conception of government, which is paternal, and which
assumes that the people are not quite competent
to manage their own affairs.   It overlooks natural
differences in money and ignores a fundamental law

[1] Thomas Paine.

which requires that, for efficient service, money must be acceptable to the people using it, and adaptable to their occupations. If we would understand the nature of money, we must get rid of the idea that mysterious complexities are inherent in it ; we must realize that it is but an implement of exchange, and no more sacred than the pound weight or the bushel measure. These complexities have so long obscured the real nature and function of money that they have come to be regarded by not a few as principles, whereas they are only obstructions to the progress of natural law. What is the Gresham law but a protest against artificial obstruction ? If there had been no bi-metallism we should never have heard of a Gresham law; if there had been no legal-tender enactment we should never have heard either of bi-metallism or mono-metallism, and when the delusive idea of regulating the value of money by legal enactment shall be dismissed, we shall have heard the last of legal tender.

Free-metallism is, therefore, what is needed. Our money must be free before it can yield to the nation its highest measure of productiveness. If the State of Colorado wants silver money, it is to the interest of the other States that she should have it. If the South could have the free silver she desires, her

industries would doubtless greatly profit thereby.
It is through individual selection, individual enterprise and competition, that we, as a people, now
excel in industrial appliances, and it is only by these
means that we shall ever excel in money.   Industrial implements vary, and individual opinions may
differ as to their respective merits, but the final
test of each implement is its adaptability for productiveness, and the necessity to secure the best is
constantly felt by the industrial producer.   The
negro has signified his preference for silver dollars
over paper or gold money, and we may be sure his
industry will be stimulated by letting him have the
money of his choice.   Silver is the choice of a par-
tially civilized race, which is shown also by the
Berbers of Algeria, who, in exchanging at Algiers
notes of the Bank of France, receive and carry to
their homes in the interior the greatly depreciated
silver in preference to the more portable gold.   To
these people bulk is a desideratum ; therefore, silver
is the money of their choice and satisfies their sense
of security, which is always essential to the efficiency
of money.   Individual preferences, however mistaken, are not crimes to be punished nor vices to be
prohibited by coercive legislation.   They stimulate
enterprise, and whatever errors of judgment they

may contain, time and experience will correct. With free scope and the incentive of profit, the monetary movement must be forward ; it cannot be otherwise.

If we will look at the silver question from the standpoint of the natural law of money, we shall find that it is a mere struggle as to whether silver or gold shall be the monetary standard of the nation. Professedly both parties advocate bi-metallism, but bi-metallism is an impossibility; it assumes that the two metals can be retained in circulation and held at a parity by the mandatory authority of the state, which, as we have seen, cannot be done. In order to hold them at a parity, the cheaper metal must be redeemable in the other ; the standard is thus practically reduced to one metal.

Now, as under bi-metallism one metal must be redeemable by the other to hold them at a parity, of what possible monetary service is the metal that has to be redeemed ? It is no longer money ; it is capital. Paper is much cheaper, and is preferable to the displaced metal, for it better fulfils the functions of money. It cannot be said that the silver held by our government serves to maintain the credit of the government's paper money ; indeed it is the fear that the paper may be redeemed in silver that has shaken the public confidence in it. Yielding no service, the silver is worse than useless where it is; for it is capital taken from the people, and thereby withheld from productive industry.

As bi-metallism is impossible, and as redeeming one metal with the other is a waste of capital, there remain but two courses to be considered : first, the adoption of one money-metal to the exclusion of the other, that is, mono-metallism ; and second, the repeal of all legal-tender laws, so that both metals may circulate independently.   This latter is the only way in which the two metals can be brought into efficient monetary service at the same time in one country.   But, it may be asked, would not this leave other commodities as well as silver and gold free to come into monetary use?   It certainly would, but their use would be governed by the law of displacement, which admits a new money only on condition that it is more efficient than that already in use. Under this natural law, it is no more necessary for a government to prescribe the kind of money that shall be used, than it is to prescribe to the house-keeper the use of the lucifer match in place of the flint and tinder-box, or to the railroad man the use of steel rails in place of iron, or to the farmer the use of the plowshare in place of the forked stick.

By a law superior to any that man can formulate, it has been a condition of industrial civilization that no advance is possible without a medium of exchange, and this condition applies to man individually, not to man in mass, for it is the individual alone who is competent to supply this medium. A proposition made recently in the Senate of the United States that aluminium shall be made a money-metal by act of Congress, indicates the prevalence among our people of an unquestioning belief in the supernatural power of legislation. The idea is simply utopian, for it is not in the power of Congress to legislate any metal, except as token-money, into general monetary use. A new metal may be used locally as money ; but it can come into general circulation only through the same slow process of natural selection that has made silver and gold the only money-metals of the civilized world ; it must establish its superior fitness over one or both of these metals, and it must have a larger open market than they have, in order to excel in stability, which is an indispensable qualification of a money-metal. Unless a new metal can stand these tests, it will not receive that individual approval that will bring it into general circulation, and even though it has all the essentials of a superior money-metal, its establishment must necessarily be of slow growth.

Hence the law of natural displacement is a sufficient bar to useless monetary innovation, and there is no need for making a money-metal legal tender; if it has superior fitness, it will circulate, and ought to circulate; if it has not, the legislation that would force it into circulation can only act as an obstruction to the introduction of better money.

The movement for silver, which seems to be favored by a majority of the people of the United States, is unquestionably based upon an honest conviction that the efficiency of our money would be enhanced by making that metal the standard of values. As, however, even under bi-metallism there is really but one standard, it is impossible to put this theory to a practical test except by expelling gold from the circulation; we have therefore no choice under bi-metallic ruling but to accept one metal or the other, or repeal all legal-tender legislation and let both metals circulate independently. With such freedom the two metals would have an even chance of proving, through individual selection, their monetary qualifications, and there is not much doubt as to what would then take place— silver would supply the needs of trade and gold the needs of commerce; the more primitive industrial localities would select silver, while the more advanced

would retain gold.   Speaking generally, the drift of
silver would be towards the industrial West and
South, and the drift of gold towards the commercial
East.   But whatever the movement of the metals
might be, we may be quite sure that each would
find for itself the employment to which it is best
adapted.

So long as bi-metallism is in force, gold must continue to be the sole monetary standard of the United
States, for the simple but sufficient reason that it is
incompatible with the genius of the American
people to work with inferior implements, and that
for this nation silver is, of the two metals, the
inferior monetary implement.   In this age of refinement of commercial methods, even gold is found to
be cumbersome, and every expedient that banker and
merchant can devise is adopted to avoid the necessity of handling it.   How foolish it is then to suppose that a money twenty-seven times heavier can,
by legislative enactment, be made to displace that
which has been the nation's standard for fifty-nine
years !   When the natural law of progression shall
be inverted, when men shall seek to increase their
burdens and to carry twenty-seven pounds to
accomplish a purpose that one pound will serve,
such legislation may be made effective, but not till

then. Such a law might be passed and be made operative for a time, but trade customs would soon prove themselves more powerful than legislative enactments. It is only by studying something of the industrial forces that are at work impelling civilization forward that we can be brought to comprehend the profounder meanings of the Silver movement, than which no great popular uprising has ever been more unfortunate in its leadership.

We believe it to be a fair presumption that before the passage of the Sherman Act in 1890, a majority of the people of the United States had accepted the fundamental doctrine of the Silverite leaders that "there is not gold enough in the world to supply the money need," and that there had been still more general acceptance of the idea that silver, being a native product, should be made our monetary standard. Why then has not this idea been put into practice? Obviously because the leaders of the movement have lost the moral warrant of their leadership. If the two metals had retained a marketable ratio of sixteen to one, the experiment of a silver monetary standard might have been made with the very general consent of the people ; but as, when the relative value of the two metals changed, the leaders made no effort to prevent injustice to individuals through the change from the gold to a silver standard, their support naturally fell away from them. In changing the standard it was the duty of these leaders to see that money issued at a gold valuation should be redeemed at a gold valuation; their claim that the change in relative value had been produced by an advance in gold rather than by a decline in silver, even if well-founded, did not lessen this obligation, nor were they relieved from it by their further claim, inconsistent with the first, that free coinage would restore silver to the standard ratio of sixteen to one of gold.

Of course it is assumed that these leaders understood that the forcible injectment of silver into the currency would ultimately expel gold from the circulation. This monetary law is so firmly established, and is so generally understood and accepted, that it is incredible they would seek shelter from responsibility on the plea of ignorance of its workings. If, on the other hand, their design was to retain both metals in circulation, as some at least of them have professed, then their duty was to have the government definitely and specifically committed to hold the two metals at a parity by making the coins interchangeable, not at the option of the Secretary of the Treasury, but at the option of the holder.   To arbitrarily redeem gold money in anything but gold, is repudiation.

A silver monetary standard would place the nation under some disadvantages ; by depriving the higher departments of industry of the more effective implement, the productive powers of the whole people would to some extent be disabled ; but if the change from gold to silver were made, as it might be, without entailing injustice upon individuals, no discredit could attach to the nation.   Capital would not then have occasion to seek, in other parts of the world, the protection it is entitled to here : it is not an objection to silver money that is frightening capital away, but the anticipation that loss of capital will result from the change of standard.   While it is true that the kind of money used by a nation indicates, as its other industrial implements do, the stage of civilization it has reached, nobody would hesitate to trade with us because of our silver money, any more than they would if our plows were forked sticks. Silver is as definite and as comprehensible a money as gold ; its cumbersomeness and instability would be our burden, and not that of those who traded with us.   Estimated by the economic intelligence of our age, our movement would be retrogressive ; but having shown a sensitive respect for the rights

10

of individuals, that general sense of security which is indispensable to industrial prosperity, instead of being weakened by the change, could not fail to be strengthened by the manifestation of a determined disposition to be honest in the making of it. Under such conditions we should doubtless, as a nation, prosper with a silver currency; nor would it be a backward step from a position of uncertainty as to which metal is to be the standard; but as compared to having a fixed gold standard, the adoption of a silver standard would be a backward step. This being the tendency of the Silver movement under its present leadership, the question naturally arises, why should a rich and resourceful nation like ours, at peace with the whole world and foremost in industrial appliances, voluntarily lower its monetary standard to the level of that of Russia and Mexico?

The argument of the leaders, that our monetary embarrassments proceed from a scarcity of gold, doubtless represents fairly the honest conviction of the great body of the supporters of the movement. We fail to understand this movement if we suppose that it proceeds merely from a desire to protect the silver-mining industry; or that it has for its object the relief, by a dishonest settlement, of the farmer's mortgage indebtedness; nor do we realize the character of the movement if we imagine it settled by the repeal of the purchase clause of the Sherman Act. That a great popular agitation should have endured for fifteen years, gathering supporters from the two regularly organized national parties, and threatening the disruption of both, proves it the possessor of at least two of the elements of political vitality that give birth to parties :—a grievance to redress that is national in character, and the coherent principle of honesty. Without these two elements a movement of such magnitude would be impossible ; it doubtless has also some elements of sordid selfishness— what popular movement has not ? It may even have individuals in the ranks of leadership who, for personal gain, would not hesitate to betray their country into the commission of a crime ; but that the rank and file of the movement, including a majority of the leaders, are working for what they believe are the best interests of the nation, it is no concession to admit, for it is a logical sequence.

Acknowledging then the honest intent of the Silver movement, we shall be better able to appreciate its earnestness and force if we will look at the subject from the Silverites' standpoint, though we cannot agree with them that there is not gold enough in the world for monetary requirements, and that, in

consequence of the supposed scarcity, a gold standard gives to the East a monopolistic power over the
West and South ; nor, that it is because of this supposed advantage that the moneyed interest of the
East is contesting for the gold standard.   But to
reject the views of the Silver party, does not prevent
our perceiving that it has more sincerity in its composition than either of the two national parties ;
while it has pressed its claims with persistent
courage, both the Democratic and the Republican
party have evaded the issue until the country has
been brought into such distress that compromise or
postponement of action is no longer possible.

It must be acknowledged that the South and West
have been overtaxed by monopolistic money ; but
this chiefly because it is government money.   It is
undoubtedly a disadvantage to be forced to use gold
in a locality where silver is more adaptable, and *vice
versa* ; yet no special advantage can accrue to either
locality from compelling the other to adopt its
money.   As all sections of our country are interde-
pendent, the prosperity of one contributes in some
measure to the prosperity of all ; hence money found
to be most effective in a given locality is the money
that should be used there, and it is also the money

that will be used if not arbitrarily interfered with. With freedom there can be no monopolistic money.

None of the Silverite leaders has attempted to state specifically in what way the country would be benefited by the change advocated; in undertaking so serious a work as the adoption of a new monetary standard, these leaders should substantiate their claim that gold is monopolistic money and that silver is not, and should also clearly define what other monetary advantages they believe to belong to silver. If instead of a change in the standard of values they had proposed a change in the standard of lineal measurement,—as for example to shorten the yard-stick to twenty inches,—they would have felt under obligation to state their reasons for wanting the change, and to state them in terms that ordinarily intelligent people could understand. They are doubtless sensible of the fact that before they could succeed in changing the yard measure, they would have to show that a yard-stick of thirty-six inches is not adapted to the arm's reach, and that one of twenty inches would facilitate the measurement of cloths, and thus save time and labor. Why then have they not clearly demonstrated how time and labor could be economized and productiveness

increased by a change in the monetary standard,—
for that is the essence of the whole question? If
they had attempted to show this, they would have
found that one is no more susceptible of demonstra-
tion than the other, yet both questions are equally
susceptible of practical, common-sense treatment.
If gold money is monopolistic, there should be no
trouble in showing specifically why it is so, for money
of any kind is not a mystery ; it is as much a tangible,
every-day, working implement as the yard-stick.

The truth is that in the popular discussion of the
Silver question, money and capital have usually
been treated as one and the same thing, and the
mystical idea of money has so obscured the general
perception as to prevent the application of the com-
monest rules of logic to the subject. Upon this
idea our whole monetary legislation is based, and
from it has sprung such a crop of complexities and
inconsistencies that it is no wonder people who have
not time to make a special study of the subject cannot realize that the natural law of money is very
simple. But though our people may be behind in
monetary science, they are quick to learn, and now
that popular interest is thoroughly awakened in the
subject, we may look with confidence for a full
solution of the problem. Justice requires that we

should not forget that a whole generation of education on this subject was lost to the people of the United States while slavery, and the adjustments growing out of its abolishment, occupied the forum of public debate to the exclusion of all other questions. It was during this period of strife and pressing need of capital that our medium of exchange passed from its natural channels of development into the control of the national government, where it has ever since been held in political bondage.

CHAPTER VIII.

THE HOARDING PANIC OF JULY, 1893.

PROBABLY most persons who were in the United States in the summer of 1893 were conscious that a great commercial crisis had arrived, but many of them may not have realized that this crisis included two distinct panics referrible to quite different causes. The first of these occurred in May, the second in July. The May panic was the culmination of a long-continued drain upon the capital of the country by foreign investors who distrusted our ability, under existing legislation, to maintain the gold standard; there was no scarcity of money at the time. Gold had already disappeared from general circulation, and was paid out only at the United States Treasury; but, notwithstanding the withdrawal of gold, the money in circulation, had it possessed the requisite elasticity, would have been sufficient in quantity to effect all exchanges in all parts of the country. The July panic was quite a different thing; it was occasioned by the hoarding of paper-money, which reduced the quantity in circulation far below the needs of the people. It is to this second panic that we wish to call special attention, because it furnishes, on the one hand, a practical illustration of the inability of a government to perform properly those functions of banking which our government has assumed in undertaking to supply the medium of exchange, and because, on the other hand, it illustrates the entire ability of the people to properly provide such a medium for themselves.

The withdrawal of capital from the country and of gold from the circulation, which preceded the May panic, were the acts of individuals who foresaw the disastrous consequences that would follow a suspension of gold payment; but that the hoarding of paper-money which brought on the panic of July was the work of individuals who were ignorant of monetary principles, is proved by the fact that the money they hoarded, like all the money in general circulation at the time, was liable to decline to the silver basis. Greenbacks are payable in coin, and coin means either silver or gold; silver certificates are payable in silver only; Treasury notes are payable in either silver or gold ; and national-bank notes may be redeemed in either greenbacks or Treasury notes.   These four kinds of paper-money, together with the silver coin in current use, constituted the entire circulating medium when the hoarding began, and the Secretary of the Treasury could at his discretion have lawfully reduced it all to a silver basis.

This entire volume of currency was substantially without elasticity ; aside from the four and a half million dollars' monthly output required by the Sherman Act, the paper-money could only be legally expanded by the issuance of notes, to the full amount of the authorized limit, by such national banks as had not already their full quota in circulation ; but to so expand it involved a preliminary outlay of capital by these banks in the purchase of government bonds, as well as a delay of from twenty to thirty days before they could get their notes from the government ; indeed, many of the applicants for notes did not receive them until after the need for them had passed.   The only other available resource left open to the people in this extreme emergency was the importation of gold ; to make any paper-money was a penal offence.

It should be borne in mind that there is, under existing laws, a tax of ten per cent. upon every form of paper, excepting government notes and national-bank notes, that may be used as a common medium of exchange in any part of the country. This tax is not levied for revenue, but is intended to suppress the issuance of any and all paper-money not directly authorized by Congress; it is, therefore, in no proper sense a tax,—it is a fine.

In attributing the first panic to the withdrawal of capital from the country, and the second to the withdrawal of money from the circulation, it is understood that these withdrawals were but the logical sequences of that monetary legislation which was the primary and sole cause of both panics. The natural conditions were all favorable to industrial growth and prosperity.

The withdrawal of capital from the country had lowered prices, it had raised the normal interest rate, it had checked new industrial undertakings, it had, in short, lowered the productive powers of the nation, thus compelling individual economy and lessening the consumption of commodities: but although, in consequence of the loss of capital, the industry of the nation could move only on a lower plane of activity, the industrial organism itself was still intact. The hoarding of the currency, on the contrary, threatened a disruption of this industrial organism, because any civilized community deprived of its medium of exchange, is thereby carried back to primitive barter. It is no more possible for a people to maintain their industrial activities without a medium of exchange, than it is for a farmer without farming implements to till the soil and produce crops.

The hoarding of paper-money doubtless began some time before its disturbing effects were seriously felt. Just before the July panic, it was noted by New York city bankers that the volume of current money in that city was shrinking at the rate of a million dollars a day, and this startling fact made it necessary for them to adopt measures to ward off the danger that threatened them ; for although a bank may be ever so solvent, it must, under a strict ruling of our national banking laws, meet its demand obligations in lawful money, or close its doors. Consequently, although this hoarding originated with persons who were ignorant of monetary principles, it soon became necessary, as a matter of self-preservation, that banks and persons who perfectly understood these principles, should refrain, as far as possible, from paying out currency. The savings banks were not only admonished to increase their reserve money, but also to keep it in their own vaults, thus withdrawing from current use the money usually kept by them in commercial banks.

The strain upon the industrial activities of the nation caused by the hoarding, reached its greatest tension in the third week of August. Congress had then been sitting in extra session for about two weeks, yet, notwithstanding the urgent appeals from all parts of the country, that body had done nothing to relieve the nation from its distress. The repeal, on the first of November, of the silver-purchase clause of the Sherman Act, served to allay the public fear of gold suspension, and doubtless somewhat checked the drain of capital from the country; but before this repeal was enacted, and while it was still the general belief that the clause would not be repealed, industries that had suspended in consequence of the hoarding, resumed operations solely through individual action, and without the least aid from Congress.

It may be doubted whether any people were ever placed in a more trying and critical position by false monetary legislation than were the people of the United States during the months of July and August, 1893, and no person at all conversant with monetary principles, noting what then took place, can fail to be impressed by the promptitude with which the

American people met the crisis and overcame it. Without any warning or previous indication, the mania for hoarding had broken out and had spread like an epidemic all over the country. Mills and factories with ample capital and in active operation, for lack of current money had to shut down and leave their work-people without employment; many perfectly solvent banks had to close their doors; railroad companies could not obtain the necessary money to pay the wages of their workmen.

Within four weeks after the July panic, the want of a medium of exchange had reduced the productive activities of the nation about thirty per cent. This was made evident by a thirty per cent. reduction in the sum-total of bank clearings in those cities which have the clearing-house system. There are eighty such cities in the United States, and the sum-total of the daily business transacted through the banks of each city is each day brought into one set of books, and the rise or fall of this sum-total, in all the cities, indicates from day to day, with measurable accuracy, the rise or decline of industrial activity in the nation at large.

The country was only saved from a much more serious crash by the action of the people who promptly took into their own hands the supplying of a medium of exchange, ignoring the laws that make such action a penal offence. Before the hoarded money had returned to the circulation, mills and factories that had shut down, started up again with a money of their own making, which their employés were satisfied to take, and which the local storekeepers freely received at its full face value in exchange for goods. To relieve their need of currency, many banks imported gold at an extra cost; forty million dollars were thus imported in August. The bank clearing-houses in the different cities issued certificates which were used among themselves in lieu of legal money in making their exchanges. About forty million dollars, in certificates of five thousand dollars each, were issued by the New York Clearing-House; while in some other cities certificates for as small a sum as ten dollars were issued, and these passed into the current circulation of the localities where they were issued.

The individual bank-check was, however, the chief instrumentality of relief in this exigency; it became for a time the common medium of exchange, as was shown by the fact that legal money was bought and sold as any commodity might be. As much as four and a half per cent. premium was paid in check-money for legal money. In these transactions, it was noted that the government paper-money some-times brought half per cent. more than gold coin, and this circumstance was interpreted by some as evidence that silver money was preferred to gold, but it had no significance beyond the fact that the silver money was paper and the gold was coin. The paper-money commanded the higher premium only because it is more convenient to handle than coin. The question of quality did not enter into these transactions. What the buyers wanted was any-thing that could legally perform the function of a medium of exchange, and they were obliged to pay a premium to obtain it because the government, in its capacity of banker-in-chief, had failed to supply this medium.

The hoarded currency began to return to the cir-culation in September, and in October the banks were amply supplied with legal money and were paying it out freely. We cannot know to what extent the extemporized money—such as bank-checks, clearing-house certificates, pay-roll checks, etc.—supplied the deficiency occasioned by the hoarding of the legal medium of exchange, but we do know that by the second week of October the industry of the nation was no longer restricted by the want of such a medium. The issuance of cer-

tificates by the New York Clearing-House, which
began in the third week of June, had reached the
sum of $38,280,000 on August 29th, and this was the
largest sum outstanding at any one time, although
there had been a total issue of $41,490,000. The
cancellation of these certificates began in the second
week of September, and the last certificate was can-
celled on the first day of November. The date of
issuance of these certificates not only enables us to
fix definitely the duration of the hoarding period,
but also to fix the time at which the strain was
greatest; this was in August, as is confirmed by the
fact that the premium on legal money began to be
paid in the second week of August and ceased with
the first week of September.

Under a monetary system that would not interfere
with the freedom of metallic money or with the
freedom of banks in the exercise of their legitimate
function of issuing paper-money, and with laws that
would recognize the vital importance of personal
supervision and individual responsibility, this hoarding panic would not have been possible; but under
our present system of government money, we are
constantly exposed to similar experiences. Nor
would this risk be lessened by a change of standard.
Whether silver or gold, or whether both these metals,

formed the standard, government paper-money would still have all its present defects; it would still have a tendency to desert the agricultural districts for the great cities, where it would stimulate unwholesome speculation; it would still be monopolistic, in the sense that it would confer upon wealth the power to create a monopoly in money. A few rich men, by withdrawing money from the circulation and locking it up, can break prices and embarrass legitimate trade, thus producing conditions in a given locality similar to those produced by the hoarder in the nation at large.

During the greenback period, this method of manipulating the New York stock market was so commonly practised that it came to be regarded almost as a legitimate occupation. A clique of moneyed men would sell a long line of securities, then put away the greenbacks received for them, and having by this means broken the market, they would buy back their securities at the reduced rates, —a transaction made possible by the lack of elasticity inherent in government paper-money.

Money is so important a factor in the creation of wealth that until we can have a paper currency with sufficient elasticity, not only to respond promptly to legitimate demands in every section of the country, but to return to its issuers for redemption when that demand shall cease, we can neither know what the productive powers of the nation are, nor can they be developed to their fullest extent; but we shall never have such a currency so long as the national government continues to exercise the function it has assumed of supplying the common medium of exchange.

INDEX.

COSIMO CLASSICS

COSIMO is an innovative publisher of books and publications that inspire, inform and engage readers worldwide. Our titles are drawn from a range of subjects including health, business, philosophy, history, science and sacred texts. We specialize in using print-on-demand technology (POD), making it possible to publish books for both general and specialized audiences and to keep books in print indefinitely. With POD technology new titles can reach their audiences faster and more efficiently than with traditional publishing.

➤ **Permanent Availability:** Our books & publications never go out-of-print.

➤ **Global Availability:** Our books are always available online at popular retailers and can be ordered from your favorite local bookstore.

COSIMO CLASSICS brings to life unique, rare, out-of-print classics representing subjects as diverse as *Alternative Health, Business and Economics, Eastern Philosophy, Personal Growth, Mythology, Philosophy, Sacred Texts, Science, Spirituality* and much more!

COSIMO-on-DEMAND publishes your books, publications and reports. If you are an Author, part of an Organization, or a Benefactor with a publishing project and would like to bring books back into print, publish new books fast and effectively, would like your publications, books, training guides, and conference reports to be made available to your members and wider audiences around the world, we can assist you with your publishing needs.

Visit our website at www.cosimobooks.com to learn more about Cosimo, browse our catalog, take part in surveys or campaigns, and sign-up for our newsletter.

And if you wish please drop us a line at info@cosimobooks.com. We look forward to hearing from you.

www.ingramcontent.com/pod-product-compliance
Lightning Source LLC
Chambersburg PA
CBHW031959190326
41520CB00007B/299